VANISHING PARADISE
THE TROPICAL RAINFOREST

VANISHING PARADISE
THE TROPICAL RAINFOREST

The Overlook Press
Woodstock · New York

First published in the United States 1990 by

The Overlook Press
Lewis Hollow Road
Woodstock
New York 12498

Library of Congress Cataloging-in-Publication Data

Dalton, Stephen
    The vanishing paradise/photographed by Stephen Dalton and
    George Bernard; written by Andrew Mitchell.
        p.   cm.
    Includes bibliographical references.
    1. Rain forest ecology – South America.   2. Rain forests – South
    America.   3. Rain forest ecology.   4. Rain forests.   I. Bernard,
    George, 1949–   II. Mitchell, Andrew, 1937–   .   III. Title.
    QH111. D35   1990
    574.5′2642′098 – dc20   90–30781
                                                   CIP

    ISBN 0–87951–406–X

This book was designed and produced by John Calmann & King Ltd, London

Designed by Mikhail Anikst
Typeset by Fakenham Photosetting Ltd, Fakenham, Norfolk
Printed in Singapore by Toppan Ltd.

The photograph on page 10 is © The Select Agency/Herbie Girardet. All
other photographs in the book may be obtained from:
    NHPA
    Little Tye
    High Street
    Ardingly
    Sussex

Stephen Dalton
George Bernard

written by
Andrew Mitchell

Contents

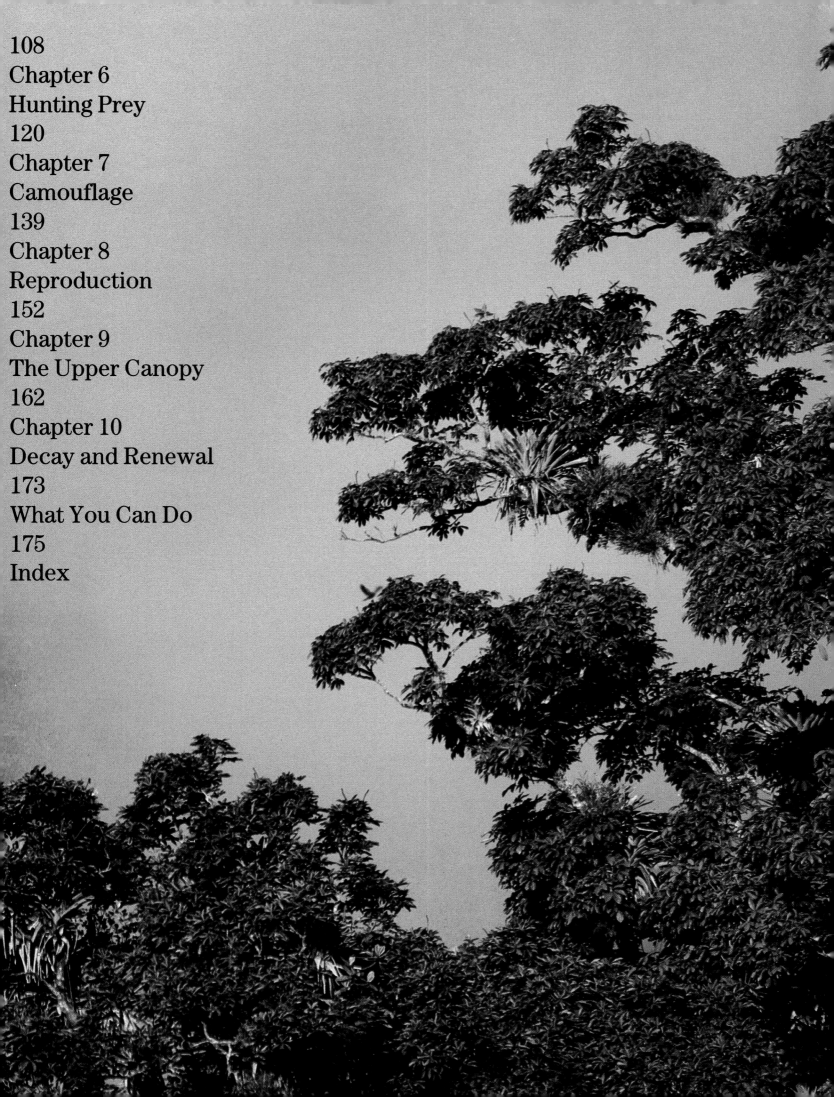

The Awakening Forest

As dawn approaches, the crowns of the giant trees are great mounds in the darkness, blacker than the night. They seem as old as history, spreading a latticework of branches and flickering leaves across a lightening sky. In the pre-dawn cold of the canopy, creatures wait for the sun. A little lower down in the forest a male howler monkey sits on a moss-covered branch high above the forest floor, and stiffly stretches a shaggy forelimb to scratch at the chocolate-coloured fur under his chin. Filling his throat sac to bursting point he roars defiance across the canopy, and his call is taken up by other members of the troop, until the forest fills with sound.

A gentle breeze ruffles the leaves of the enchanted canopy as the early morning cicadas begin to rasp and whine like a symphony of tiny chain saws. An enormous sphinx moth unfurls its long proboscis and probes a large white flower. It is empty: bats have already passed this way in the night, hovering in front of the flowers, and licking nectar with their long tongues tipped with nectar-gathering papillae. To the east, the sky begins to change colour from indigo to lighter blue, slowly revealing the jagged edges of the mountains. As the first rays of sunshine creep around a mountain's edge and lance across the forest roof, the leaves appear to catch fire. Dull greys and dark shadows recede into the forest as the leaves dance with light, flashing gold and magenta, blazing with oranges and yellows. The sun rises higher, washing stars and red clouds from the sky, and the canopy transforms into a multitude of greens. In these valleys an exuberance of life has existed for thousands of years.

An awakening such as this might happen in any pristine tropical rainforest in South America – from Southern Mexico, through Central America, across the mighty Amazon basin to the northern hills of Bolivia. This region of the globe is still home to the greatest diversity of life in the Americas and possibly in the world. The term 'rainforest' is to some extent a misnomer, as in many so-called rainforests it does not rain for months at a time. Some forests look like jungles but are quite dry. Rainforests flourish best in lowland tropical areas ten degrees north and south of the equator, where rainfall is frequent and the air feels humid and blood-warm. Soils, too, alter the character of the forest. Where they are tainted with minerals or are naturally acid, only certain trees grow, leaving the forest starved of both plant and animal variety.

Moving from lowlands to mountains the forest changes again. Short gnarled trees draped in moss exist in the cool of high mountains. The birds, insects and mammals that live here are quite different from those inhabiting the lofty trees in the lowlands of the Amazon basin. Some of these may be taller than a ten-storey building. There are still other kinds of rainforest. In those that grow in the mighty *vareza*, the plains of Brazil, the Amazon floodwaters spread through mile upon mile of the forest each year, enabling fish to glide between buttress roots where land animals usually roam. The fish gulp seeds falling from the branches above, so that the trees have evolved to rely on them to distribute their offspring.

In such tropical hothouse environments rainforests support the greatest diversity of life on earth. In just one acre, two hundred different species of tree may grow. In the whole of Britain there are under twenty native species. One rainforest tree may contain over fifty species of ant and ten thousand other species of insects, spiders and mites. The rainforest canopy alone may contain half of all species of life on earth. In the last few years the extent of our ignorance has become obvious as scientists have begun to probe that last biological frontier. Biologists have discovered that it is the exception rather than the rule to find an insect in the canopy which has been given a name and a classification. The discoveries in the last decade have been so numerous that the original estimates of the number of insect species in the world has had to be revised upwards from one million to thirty million. It is as if naturalists have at last stumbled on nature's Tutankhamun: as we scrape away at the treasure chamber and glimpse its riches, the feeling grows that we are staring into a tomb.

Try snapping your fingers once every second. In the time it takes for the noise of each snap to disperse, an acre of rainforest will have disappeared for ever. Central Park in New York would take about sixteen minutes. A rainforest area the size of Britain is destroyed annually in the Brazilian forest burning season. In a generation an area the size of India will be wiped out unless a new, sustainable way of using these forests can be devised. At the current rate of destruction, the world's lowland forests have only twenty years left.

Thirty per cent of the world's rainforests are in the Brazilian Amazon, while West Africa now contains just under twenty-five per cent, half of which is in Zaire. South-East Asia houses the majority of the remainder, home to orang-utans, gibbons and birds of paradise, but also some of the world's most heavily harvested timber forests. Australia is the only western nation to possess its own tropical rainforest, on the Cape York Peninsula. The myriad Pacific Islands contain some of the world's most endangered animals in unique forests which have evolved isolated from land. Today, rainforests cover less than eight per cent of the world's surface, somewhat less than half of their original area since man began exploiting them.

In Amazonia there is still a huge area of forest left, but this is no reason for complacency. Despite all the efforts of conservation groups worldwide and pressure from western governments, the pace of destruction is quickening. Each year the burning season covers a larger area. In the frontier towns of the Amazonian wilderness the air can grow so thick with smoke that car headlamps must be lit during the day and handkerchiefs used to cover mouths in an atmosphere of perpetual twilight. The forest crackles to the sound of exploding trunks and reeks of roasted creatures, and as the stench of death fills the air, eagles, owls and parrots flee across a blackened sky. As pioneer farmers wield chain saws, timber bleeds its accumulated wealth into the thin soil, and soon it is washed away into already muddy rivers, to clog dams and threaten coastal fishing communities hundreds of kilometres away.

Rainforests across the world are fighting their last stand. In West Africa countries such as the Ivory Coast have lost some ninety per cent of their forest. This, a legacy of colonial times, has left their prospects for future development crippled. In all Africa, only Zaire has large areas of pristine woodland left. In Asia too, great swathes are being cut through the forests of Sumatra, Borneo and New Guinea. Those of peninsular Malaysia are all but gone and recently Thailand banned logging for lack of wood. Even in northern Australia, roads are cut through forest areas as developers jostle for a slice of the green cake: the breathtaking scenery brings tourist dollars.

Why is this carnage happening? The reasons seem almost as varied as the forest itself. Simply put, the most desperate and damaging intrusions are caused by farmers from outside the forest who have no land on which to grow crops to feed their children, and so move into the forest to create shortlived farms and a mirage of prosperity. A more complex cause is debt. Selling timber or raising cattle on cleared land brings in badly needed foreign exchange which helps developing nations to meet the crippling interest payments on debts to western banks. Indigenous tribes, the true guardians of the forest, have over centuries evolved an efficient method of using the forest on a sustainable basis. It is known as 'slash and burn' agriculture. A small area is felled for family or village use and burned. The ash provides fertilizer for a variety of crops for a few years and then a new area is chosen, leaving the previously cleared area to regrow. This form of management relies on a small population and large areas of forest. Today's increasing population has made this system impossible.

Since the Second World War the landless poor of Brazil, crowded in city fringe slums, have proved an enduring embarrassment to local politicians. What better than to open up a new 'wild west' in the provinces of Acre and Rondonia in which these people could find new hope? In the 1970s and the early '80s the World Bank and other international lending agencies provided finance for roads to get them there. Roads were cut through Indian lands without protecting Indian rights adequately and so a tide of destruction by enthusiastic farmers, who knew far too little about the ways of the forest, was unleashed. Some eight million hectares of forest continue to be destroyed in this way each year. The land promised to these pioneers and intended to support them for generations soon becomes infertile and they have no choice but to move on, cutting deeper into the forest. Cattle ranchers follow, buying the cleared land cheaply and making easy money from beef cattle which they graze on the stump-strewn grasslands and sell to American fast-food interests. Almost three-quarters of Brazil's cleared forest is used for cattle ranching but within ten years the soil is filled with weeds – a barren and wasted desert which is not even good enough for grazing.

Almost as great a threat to the rainforests is logging. There is a worldwide market for hardwood timber and paper pulp. Hardwoods are used extensively in the construction industry, in furniture making, even for chopsticks in Japan. Forty per cent of world exported tropical hardwoods enter Japan, making it the single greatest exploiter of rainforests in the world. One of the most valuable acts of conservation in the world today would be to encourage the Japanese to use the natural resources of other nations as wisely as they use their own. Their commercial destruction of Asian rainforests, whilst leaving their own extensive timber resources alone, is an assault on the environment from which the planet will never recover. The timber importers of America and Europe also should ensure that they buy only those rainforest products that are produced sustainably.

Another cause of destruction in South America is mining. Vast quantities of iron ore lie beneath the forests. No developing country can afford either to leave them there, or to mine them without destroying the forest. Brazil alone plans to burn 700,000 tons of charcoal a year to feed its pig-iron smelters. The need for energy to fuel these industries and the towns which support them requires electric power on a massive scale. One hundred and twenty-five hydroelectric dams are planned in Brazil by the year 2010 which could flood 25,000 hectares (60,000 acres) of forest and displace thousands of Indians living there. Fortunately, however, the World Bank, which was to approve loans for the dams and other projects, has withheld its support until environmental safeguards are improved.

Most of us are left with a sense of frustration at these events, but feel either powerless to effect change, or, worse, uninvolved. The rainforest touches few Western lives other than through newsprint and television documentaries seen by relatively small and often already committed audiences. Few of us are aware of the rainforest in our own homes, yet each day we use products bequeathed to us by them – unthinkingly. Coffee, cocoa, rubber, exotic fruits, hardwood furniture, window frames and security doors, cane chairs, even mahogany lavatory seats. Every day in our hospitals drugs developed from raw materials found in the rainforests save lives. Curare is a muscle relaxant used by Amerindians to tip their poisoned hunting darts. A derivative enables Western anaesthetists to control our breathing during surgery. The rosy periwinkle, discovered in Madagascar's forests, is often quoted for its success in treating Hodgkin's disease, resulting in eighty per cent remission. The Mexican yam, a rainforest shrub, produced the Pill. Few can deny the value of these drugs in both financial and medical terms, and they can be harvested from the forest without destroying it, yet barely one per cent of rainforest plants have been tested for their potential value to mankind. Who knows – a cure for Aids may lie in the next acre of forest to be burned.

Tropical forests also bequeath gifts on a global scale. They act as a sponge, absorbing up to three metres (ten feet) of rainfall annually, and delivering clean water to streams and rivers upon which millions of people depend. Most of the water is returned to the atmosphere, evaporating through leaf surfaces to create the billowing white clouds that sail across a green ocean of leaves. The moisture may fall on lands far beyond the forest which otherwise would have no rain. Conversely, the burning of tropical forests pollutes the atmosphere with vast amounts of carbon dioxide contributing to the greenhouse effect which could grossly alter the earth's climate within a generation.

Rainforests have often been described as the lungs of the earth. Along with plankton, they are our greatest producers of oxygen. Through the process of photosynthesis, each leaf in a rainforest acts as a miniature solar panel, converting the energy of the sun to sugars and thus absorbing carbon dioxide from the atmosphere. Although these forests scrub the air clean of one of the most significant 'greenhouse' gases, it seems unreasonable to dictate terms on their use to those countries which own them until we have put our own house in order. American automobiles eject as much carbon dioxide into the atmosphere as the current burning of Brazilian forests. The changes we ourselves have to make are as challenging as those facing Amazonia. Consumers in Japan and Europe are the market for much of the logger's wood, and so can influence its use by their buying patterns. Green consumerism and industry's growing desire to see the sustainable use of resources as good business have not come a moment too soon.

Astronauts have given us a unique picture of our blue planet with its soft white haze of atmosphere. Each night on our television screens computer-

animated pictures of cloud patterns swirling across azure oceans and earth-coloured landscapes create a living impression of the planet. In 1785 the Scottish geologist James Hutton first proposed that the earth itself actually 'lived'. Now James Lovelock, a Fellow of the Royal Society of London, has eloquently elaborated on this theme in his hypothesis of Gaianism. This revolutionary explanation of how the earth works as a giant super-organism takes its name from the Greek earth goddess Gaia. For the first time Lovelock has formulated a process through which to study the earth as a whole and in which science and religion have a common language.

To anyone who has spent a day scrambling over granite rocks, the idea that the earth could in some way be alive might seem ridiculous. However, our notion of life is challenged when gazing up at a giant rainforest tree, one of nature's largest living things. A mere ten per cent of its great trunk and branches is alive and flowing with sap; the remainder is old, lifeless wood. Lovelock believes that the earth is similarly clothed with a thin film of life and that its great limestone cliffs and sedimentary hills are merely by-products of processes initiated by living organisms in some way subordinated to the Gaian ethic of maintaining dynamic but stable conditions for life on earth.

When the planets were born, they were lifeless. Only on earth were the conditions right for respiring microbes to change a dangerous cocktail of gases into an atmosphere conducive to the flowering of a multitude of higher life forms dependent on oxygen. Gaianism declares that these life forms now regulate our climate to suit themselves. Our level of oxygen has remained at about twenty per cent for two hundred million years. If it rose above twenty-five per cent, the earth might catch fire, if it went below fifteen per cent, we would suffocate. For Gaia, it is not the individual form of life or even a whole host of species which is important, but the maintenance of an atmosphere conducive to life. Gaianism predicts that a destabilizing force will inevitably result in a rectifying reaction. Gaia both gives birth to abundant life and destroys it, as the fossil records show.

Nature does not care whether the rainforests live or die; only humans do. Any belief that one species has a right to survive over another is entirely human. The busy to and fro of human civilization is a passing moment in the long evolution of life on this planet. If our species should cut off the branch on which it is sitting, both woodman and tree would vanish, leaving only a fossil trace, but Gaia would produce others to replace them. It is presumptuous for humans to believe that we can manage the planet. Yet because we care for our own survival, we now care for the survival of the forests, and it is essential that we do so, both for ourselves and for our children's sake.

The exuberant display of life in the rainforests is captured in this book by two of the finest natural history photographers in the world. Everything that you see here could be found in one hectare of a tropical rainforest in South America. As you turn each page it will be as though you are viewing the entire evolutionary process. Around each bush, across a stream, through the rainforest, you are about to enter a world that must never be allowed to become a memory.

Warscewiczia coccinea
The red bracts of this plant attract the attention of pollenators in an otherwise green environment. Note the extraordinary number of differently shaped leaves in this fragile and diverse habitat.

1
The Atmosphere of the Forest

In the forest shortly after dawn the air smells as rich as a plum cake. It is as though you are walking through a huge botanical hothouse filled with mists and sweetly scented orchids. In the twilight zone beneath the canopy, beams of light lend shadows to vines and trunks and great walls of leaves, giving one a sense of creeping behind the scenes of an enormous theatre. There is an architecture to the forest. Trunks rise up in many forms. Some, in areas prone to flooding, stand as if on tiptoe on skeletal roots; others, where it is drier, are braced with giant buttresses, and still others form huge columns rising smoothly directly out of the ground. Small shrubs and bushes crowd the lower layers of the forest. Through them young trees struggle upwards in the relative gloom, seeking a gap through which to jostle towards the canopy above. Thirty to forty metres (up to 120 yards) above ground is the canopy layer where crowns almost interlock to create a network of branches and leaves as complex as any stained-glass window. The leaves of each crown do not touch, they merely whisper to each other across a gap. Some species, taller than the rest, break through and spread their giant crowns above the forest to soak up the sun, occasionally carrying great bursts of yellow, violet and magenta blooms. These, the mightiest of the forest trees, are known as emergents.

Creeping over the shrubby surfaces, passion flower vines display their exquisite spiky flowers of yellow, purple and violet. Our idea of the jungle as an inhospitable place filled with terrifying tribes and dangerous beasts, although it has been inherited from Victorian explorers crazed with malaria or a desire to glamourize their adventures, is still, to some extent, a true one. The forest is populated with biting insects, poisonous snakes and spiders, and jaguars with lethal jaws, but most of these are seen only rarely, and wound from fear, not malice.

It is a humbling experience to pick your way along a small path or animal track between the buttress roots of a tree as high as a ten-storey building, topped with a crown the size of a football pitch. Some trunks are clear of branches and vegetation for thirty metres, others are thickly clustered with vines, ferns, bromeliads, mosses and lichens. The view of the canopy is obscured by sub-canopy trees reaching towards the light, which is criss-crossed with a black spaghetti pattern of vines and the fanned beauty of palms.

Suddenly there might be a flash of light on a butterfly's iridescent wings or the gleam of bright reds and yellows on the beautiful plumage of an unidentifiable bird rushing by. A haze of small insects may dance in a beam of sunlight while two male butterflies flutter upwards in a shaft of light. For a second there may be pandemonium as some unseen creatures, perhaps small deer or a group of sleeping peccaries, are disturbed and make off through the undergrowth. Then the commotion dies away and the background hum of insects can be heard once more, a hum punctuated by a parrot's squawk or an occasional outbreak of twittering from a hunting party of small birds passing through the canopy overhead, collecting insects.

First impressions of the forest are often disappointing. To see what is there, you must first stop looking for it, sit quietly on a comfortable root and wait for its inhabitants to lose interest in you. At your feet you might see a scatter of giant leaves subtly coloured in browns and reds, and perhaps covered in a sheen of water from the morning's rain. Kicking them aside, a fine tangle of roots and white fungal threads is revealed, and a surprisingly thin layer of ochre-coloured soil. With bedrock just centimetres away, the roots of the mighty rainforest trees can be seen above ground level right across the forest floor. The little rainwater which reaches them is sucked up along with valuable nutrients in the mulch of decaying leaves and travels up through the trunk to the canopy. As the first rays of sunshine strike the canopy, a fog appears, apparently from the interior of the forest, and gently spirals upwards. Yet below the canopy the air is clear. The phenomenon is explained by the meeting of warm moist air, which has been trapped among the trees at night and which rises at dawn, with the cooler air above. The resulting condensation forms the mist. Within an hour or so it disperses as the sun warms the air above the forest. Through tiny pores in the leaves of the trees, moisture and oxygen escape to the atmosphere and as the day proceeds, great clouds unfold into the sky, announcing an afternoon filled with thunder, clattering rain, and gently moving rainbows.

The rainforest's ability to regulate moisture in the air is one of its greatest benefits to the world. It acts like a sponge, releasing clean water to the environment without eroding it. If the forest cover is removed, torrential rain gouges canyons in the soil, washing it into rivers, clogging dams downstream, and polluting coral reefs on the coast, often hundreds of kilometres away.

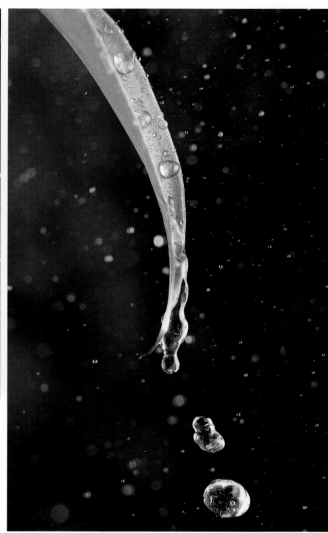

Water dripping from the 'drip tips' of a leaf onto the ground below. A vital part of the natural cycle of the forest, this process allows the plant to breathe and prevents other plants from taking root on it. Leaves are the lungs of the forest, as well as its solar panels.

The Humid Forest

A tropical storm can drop more than six centimetres (two inches) of rainfall onto the forest in an hour. Three-quarters of it may be intercepted by the canopy and the understorey and evaporated back into the atmosphere to water thirsty branches elsewhere before it ever reaches the ground. There are no raging floods on the ground because the forest drip-feeds water to the environment slowly, preventing erosion and maintaining clean, productive rivers. These controls are finely tuned and damage to world forests has reversed them, ruining rivers, clogging dams, and sweeping thousands of lives away in floods. Even individual leaves are exquisitely designed, with elongated tips which drain water from their waxy surfaces, perhaps to speed the process of drying in a world where humidity often reaches over ninety-five per cent. With abundant light, warmth and water the rainforests are one of the most productive environments on earth, but this is not always immediately apparent. The nineteenth-century naturalist Henry Bates wrote, on first entering the rainforests of Brazil, 'But where are the flowers? To our great disappointment we saw none ... There was no tumultuous movement, or sound of life. We did not see or hear monkeys, and no tapir or jaguar crossed our path.' After eleven years spent studying the forest world his view became very different.

There is very little wind in the forest; the stillness allows tall thin trees to remain upright. The night mist, which has soaked plants and animals alike, still lingers as the sun rises.

Flashes of Light

Trees are among the most effective energy converters in the
world, and sunlight is the source of energy upon which the
rainforest engine depends. Leaves act as solar panels using
chlorophyll (green pigment) within the leaf structure,
combined with carbon dioxide sipped through small pores on
the leaf surface, to make sugars. Phosphates and nitrates
garnered from decaying vegetation build proteins. This
process creates the largest living structures on earth. So
efficient are leaves at mopping up the sun that the interior of
the forest resembles a twilight zone, splashed with sunlight
burning white on the exposed surfaces of living leaves and
dappling the brown carpet of dead ones on the forest floor.

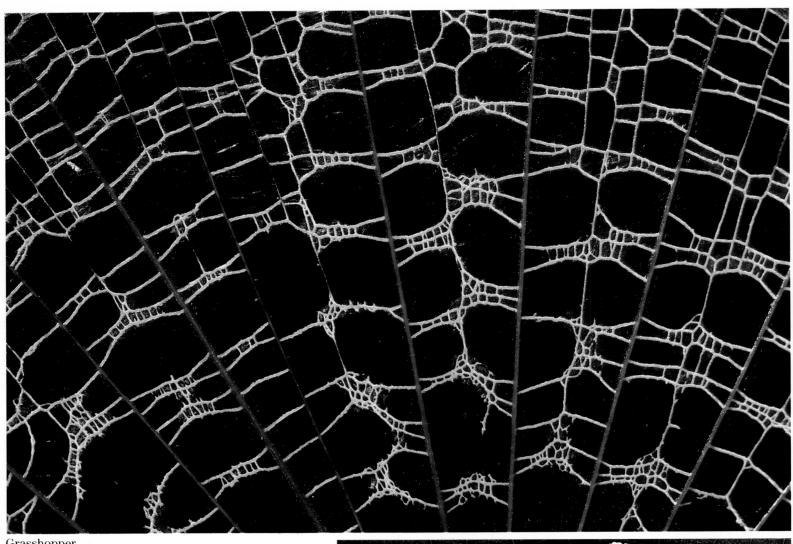

Grasshopper
(Taeniopoda maxima)
Patterns of veining on the insect's
leathery wing.

Feeding patterns on a leaf left by
leaf skeletomizer and leaf miner
insects.

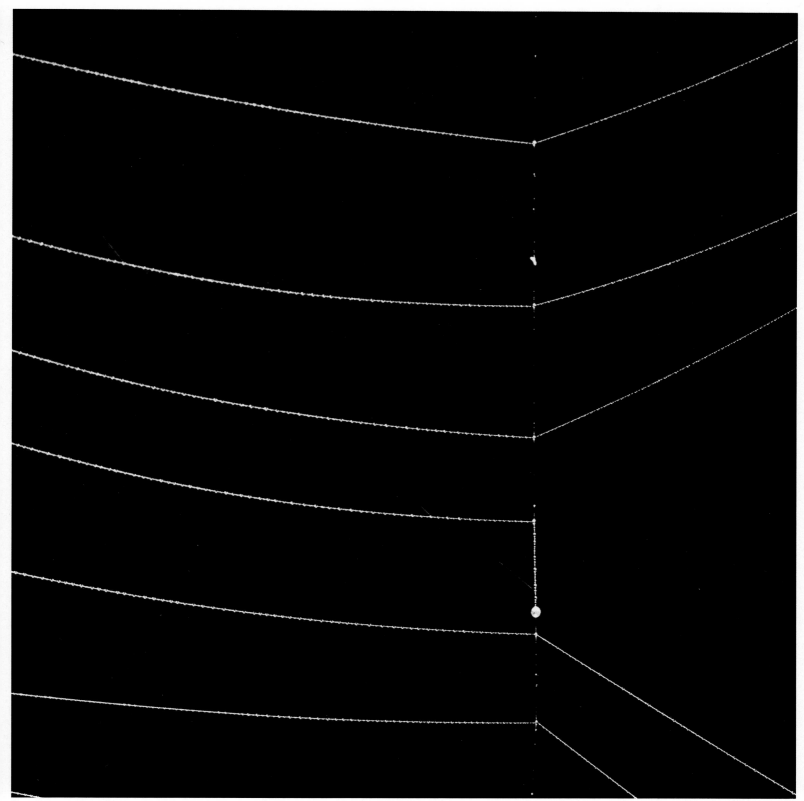

Spider's web by night

OVERLEAF, LEFT:
Palm
(Welfia georgii)
The leaves of this young plant are orange, but turn green as they mature. The theory that has been formulated for this is that, in low levels of light such as those found in the understorey, orange pigment in the immature plant absorbs light more easily than green.

OVERLEAF, RIGHT:
Tree bark
(Dussia macrophyllata)
Immature plant bugs congregating around the base of a tree, where they feed on sap with their sucking mouthparts.

Hummingbird
(Amazilia dumerilii)
The diminutive size, dazzling colours and breathtaking flying skills of these little birds, together with the mysterious humming sounds they make in flight, must have puzzled early visitors to the New World. Writing in 1632, Thomas Morton describes the hummingbird as a 'curious bird ... that out of the question lives upon the bee, which he eateth and catcheth among the flowers, for it is his custom to visit such places'. Now we know that hummingbirds visit flowers to feed on nectar, but they also need to supplement their food with small insects which are caught on the wing.

Jaguar
(Felis onca)
Larger than the African leopard, the jaguar weighs between fifty and a hundred kilos (110–220 pounds). Sadly, due to hunting and the destruction of its habitat, this beautiful creature is now a very rare find in South America. Even in reserves there is an average of only one jaguar in every hundred square kilometres (thirty-eight square miles). Solitary by nature, jaguars are very aggressive to other members of the species. They will patrol a certain area for days at a time, stalking prey which includes rodents and small tapirs. Fast both on land and in the water, they can hunt in either habitat.

Geometrid Moth
Resting on a heliconia plant, this moth is protected from predators by its camouflage, which makes it look like one dead leaf fallen on another.

Yellow-Headed Parrot
(Amazona ochrocephala)
Green amazon parrots live principally in the canopy of the forest, feeding on fruits, nuts and seeds, the shells of which they break open with their beaks. There are many species of amazons and there is little difference between the plumage of the male and the female – both are well camouflaged against predators such as hawks, buzzards and eagles.

OVERLEAF:
Grey Tree Boa
(Boa annulata)
An adult boa grows to about four metres (twelve feet) long. An agile predator living at ground level and in the understorey, it preys on birds and small mammals. It stuns the prey with a swift head-butt, coils around it to kill by suffocation, then swallows its victim whole, head first.

ABOVE:
Skipper Butterfly Pupa
(Family Hesperiidae)
At a vulnerable time for all insects, a skipper caterpillar has sewn two leaves together with silk to make a protective covering as it metamorphoses in its pupal case.

TOP:
Milkweed Butterfly Pupa
(Danaus plexippus)
After attaching itself to the underside of a leaf on its food plant, the pupa will emerge in about ten days as an adult butterfly.

Bush Cricket
(Family Tettigoniidae)
Many creatures of the forest hide away during the daylight hours, only to become active at night, feeding, fighting and mating. The shrill chirpings of crickets create a background hum which is part of the haunting night-time chorus of the forest.

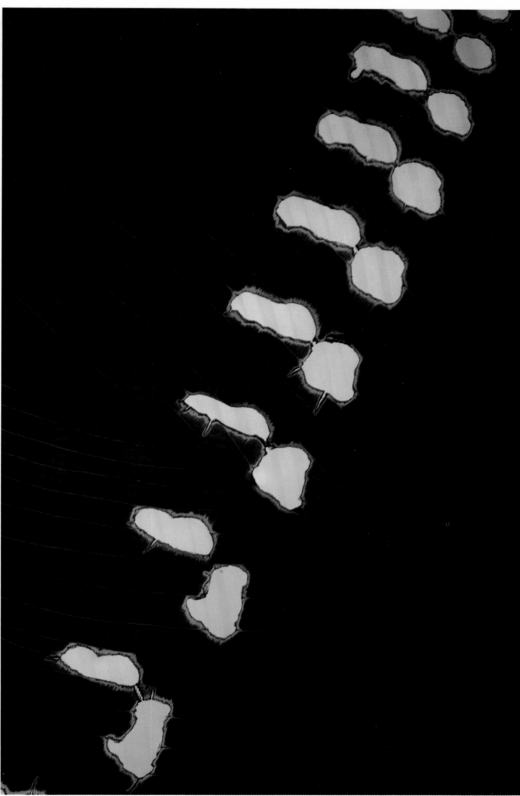

ABOVE:
Planthopper feeding
(Family Cicadellidae)
The planthopper obtains nutrients
by piercing leaves and stems with
its mouthparts and sucking the sap.

TOP:
Gecko
(Gonatodes ceciliae)
Seen from below, the gecko is
silhouetted on a leaf. It lives on the
forest floor and is seen here
sunbathing, absorbing heat before
wandering off to hunt for insects.

Heliconia Leaf
Before this leaf unfurled, a
Xenarescus beetle ate through it,
creating a pattern with the holes it
left behind.

Water Cabbage
(*Pistia stratiotes*)
Like those of the water lily, the furry leaves of this plant are water repellent, enabling it to float on the water's surface.

RIGHT:
Tropical forest stream and waterfall. It is a refreshing experience to stumble across a stream or waterfall in the heat of the forest. Water always attracts a wide variety of life.

Blackwater Rivers

Jungles are the birthplaces of mighty rivers and none is mightier than the Amazon, which contains one-fifth of all flowing fresh water on earth. A single island in its estuary is the size of Switzerland. Such is the volume of water emerging each day from its mouth that one hundred and fifty kilometres (ninety miles) into the Atlantic, Amazon waters are still sweet enough to drink. Inside the forest such rivers have small beginnings. Sometimes the water is clear, but often it is the colour of weak tea from the tannin which seeps into it from decaying leaves. The Rio Negro is aptly named. Its black waters are mostly nutrient-free due to the efficiency of the Amazonian forest at capturing the nitrates and phosphates released from decomposing leaves. Surprisingly, millions of fish survive in these blackwater rivers, despite the lack of food they offer. The fish feed on seeds which fall from the forest canopy. 64,000 square kilometres (40,000 square miles) of forest flood each year in the rainy season in Amazonia. Three-quarters of the fish sold in inland markets here depend on seeds to exist, and, in their turn, the people of the Amazon depend on the fish as their principal source of protein.

Violet-Eared Hummingbird
(Colibri thalassinus)
In order to fly efficiently, this jewel-like bird needs to keep its plumage in good order. Here it is preening and washing its feathers in a calm part of a waterfall.

LEFT:
Rivers like this are often laden with silt, a result of forest destruction further upstream. They carry away topsoil and tree-trunks, and with these, many of the forest's essential nutrients.

Caiman
(Family *Alligatoridae*)
Although crocodilians are in many respects the most highly developed of reptiles, they are also the closest existing creatures to the large prehistoric reptiles of the Mesozoic period of more than two hundred million years ago. Like crocodiles and alligators, caimans are highly predatory, feeding on fish, insects and carrion.

Heat from the sun has cleared the lower levels of the forest mist, leaving the canopy still shrouded in vapours.

The Canopy

The canopy is the real powerhouse of the forest. It is home to the greatest biomass of animals and plants, the interface between the forest and the sun. More than 10,000 different insect species have been discovered to co-exist in just one tree. A new breed of arboreal naturalist is finally exploring this frontier, using climbing ropes, aerial walkways, and even hot air balloons. Still, the upper reaches of the forest remain, for the most part, tantalizingly out of reach. The canopy promises to reveal more about life on earth than any other environment, yet even as you read this book, it is being burned at an uprecedented rate all over the world.

RIGHT:
Buttress roots. This giant tree, which stands over fifty metres (150 feet) high, has a very shallow root system in comparison with temperate forest trees. Impressive buttress roots reaching five metres (fifteen feet) up the trunk give additional support and help to stabilize the tree.

OVERLEAF:
A view of pristine forest, showing the light and shade of the understorey.

Night

In the tropics, night falls within minutes. A new shift of creatures emerges from its daytime hiding places. Bats replace birds, moths take over from butterflies, toads crawl from their lairs under the leaves, and hunters prowl the dark corridors of the forest. Owls with faces shaped like radar reflectors listen for the slightest sound made by a mouse or a lizard. Walking along a forest path one can be startled by a nightjar as it flutters up from the trail. Fifteen minutes after dusk an owl monkey with huge saucer-shaped eyes may emerge from a tangle of vines to search for insects, fruits and nectar. Night is a good time to hunt if you do not wish to be seen. To avoid the drying sun many frogs are active at night, staking out territories and singing to their mates. Occasionally they receive a chilling answer as frog-hunting bats, tuned to their song, lunge out of the darkness and scoop them from their courting grounds.

A moonlit night in the forest is advantageous to predators but disadvantageous to their prey.

ABOVE LEFT:
Click Beetle
(*Pyrophorus* sp.)
This understorey-dwelling click beetle emerges at the beginning of the rainy season. As it rests, two bio-luminescent lights on its thorax attract potential mates. It also has a ventral light which shines downwards in flight.

Sunset and moonrise over the forests of Venezuela are almost simultaneous. As the sun sinks below the horizon the darkening forest starts to fill with the sounds of frogs, crickets and other nocturnal creatures.

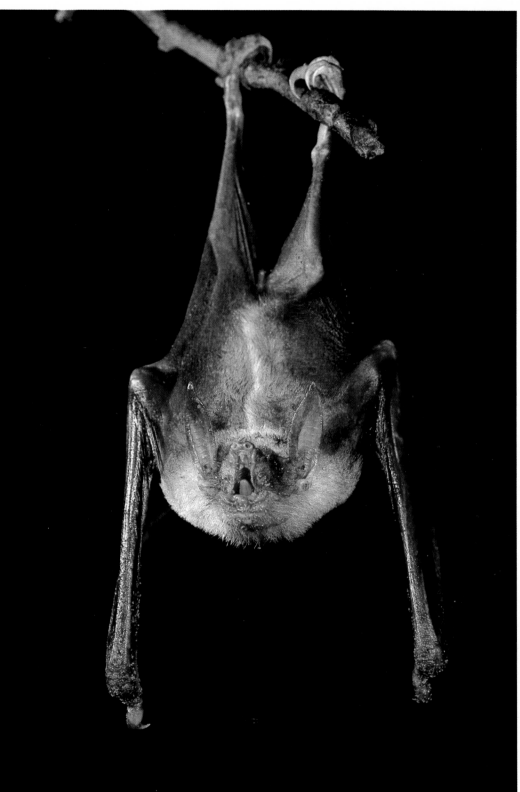

ABOVE:
Tropical Elm
(Ampelocera sp.)
The young leaves of this tropical elm are a delicate shade of silver-blue. They turn green as they mature.

TOP LEFT:
Tree Frog
(Hyla sp.)
Most tree frogs are nocturnal: this one has spent the day resting on a tree trunk, attached by means of suckers on the ends of its toes. These help it to move around the foliage by jumping from one leaf to another, sometimes catching on with only one foot. Some tree frogs are camouflaged, protecting themselves from predators by staying absolutely immobile.

Fishing Bat
(Noctilio leporina)
A roosting fishing bat. It wakes at night to hunt for food. Alerted by means of its sonic radar to ripples in the water and swooping down to trawl over the surface, it gaffs fish with its claws, kills the prey with its teeth, and eats either in flight or hanging upside-down from a branch.

2
The Variety of Life

More than half of all life on earth is believed to exist in the tree crowns of the forest. The diversity of known life is astonishing and that still waiting to be discovered is overwhelming. In the world today about one and a half million species have been described by scientists, and of these a million live in the temperate zones. Thirty million or more wait to be described in the tropics. As for cataloguing the animals and plants with which we share the earth, we have not even begun.

To the forest-watcher, each hidden root space, collection of leaves, massive hollow trunk, or crown of flowers is a whole universe of life awaiting investigation. Once, in a bromeliad plant I explored in Costa Rica, I found four brightly uniformed harvestmen streaked in yellow, a tiny brown spider brooding over some eggs, three different kinds of woodlouse, a centipede, a millepede, numerous unidentifiable small beetles, a primitive wormlike peripatus, a pseudoscorpion, some whirligig beetles spinning on trapped water inside the leaves, several chironomid fly larvae swimming under the surface, various earwigs, a tree seedling, a cockroach nymph, a nest of minute brown ants complete with eggs and larvae, some seeds attached to fluffy parachutes, mites galore, a mottled brown frog; and an earthworm with an iridescent blue nose. All these lived in a single plant which grows on tree branches high above the forest floor.

Walking through the forest it is rare to see two trees the same. An area the size of a football pitch might contain two hundred different species of tropical tree. An equivalent area in a temperate forest might have only ten. A 50-hectare (125-acre) plot in Malaysia has revealed 835 native tree species – more than in the whole of the United States. Panama has almost twice as many butterflies as the United States. The Amazon river contains some three thousand species of fish, a greater number than the whole of the Atlantic. On a dark, damp night in the rainforest a single light bulb will attract more exotic and fantastic creatures than Hollywood's most imaginative directors could ever dream up.

Where did all this diversity come from? Part of the explanation is that the rainforest contains numerous mutually distinct micro-environments available for occupation. Animals and plants segregate their lives within the immense matrix of the forest according to humidity, light, temperature, the availability of food and protection, and soil nutrients. Some insects confine themselves to the undersides of rotting leaves, others to the surface of lichens. Butterflies may occupy distinct heights in the forest from the dark understorey to the canopy, each species using its wing colours to disguise itself in various levels of light. Mosquitoes move up and down in the forest at different times of the day, whilst other insect groups are organized into layers. Some birds will remain in the shrub layer of the forest, others will occupy only the canopy. Many monkeys, mice and anteaters patrol lofty highways rarely, if ever, visiting the ground. Heavier animals, such as tapirs and jaguars, remain close to the forest floor. This separation of life means that many species can rub shoulders without stepping on each other's ecological toes. Life in the tropical forest has evolved through cooperation as well as competition.

Uniqueness is believed to evolve through isolation. It is possible that many great forests may have shrunk to islands of diversity when the world's climate cooled during the ice ages. In these isolated pockets of forest, still vast areas, new species evolved on their own. As the earth warmed, these pockets of forest expanded and converged. Evidence for this is that certain patches of Amazonia contain rich varieties of species which do not overlap with other areas. These centres of diversity are believed to be the havens which survived the ice ages and it is these areas which it is crucial to save for the future.

Biodiversity is a term used to describe the variety of life. The most varied systems are often also the most stable ones, with many checks and balances able to cope with change. The rainforest is stable but fragile: the biodiversity of the system is easily compromised. The number of species it can support drops as the forest diminishes in size. The island of Borneo will therefore sustain a greater variety of life than a small forested island in the Pacific. As deforestation leaves mere fragments of forest in Amazonia, the effect on biodiversity is catastrophic. The area of forest which a group of howler monkeys needs in order to survive is much larger than that needed by, say, an ant. If vast forests are reduced to mere patches the exuberance of life inevitably diminishes. How big should a reserve be to maintain a population of jaguars and the adequate balance of prey? Which trees must remain to provide fruit for scarlet macaws in the dry season? Which bee is the pollen messenger that ensures a tree's survival by fertilizing others of its kind? The answers to these kinds of questions are crucial if we are to understand how to keep the forests alive and healthy.

PREVIOUS PAGE:
There may be as many as two hundred species of tree in every hectare of the rainforest, while the variety of animal life probably reaches tens of thousands of species.

Stilt Palm
(Socratea durissima)
Many species of trees, particularly in wet areas, have evolved stilt roots to give them added support. When hunting, Amazonian Indians use the hollowed-out stilts of this palm as blow-pipes for darts tipped either with the plant-based muscle-relaxant curare, or the toxic mucus of poison-dart frogs.

Liverwort Moss
The fruiting bodies of this moss create a miniature jungle within the forest.

Epiphytes
(Family Araceae)
Epiphytes living in the understorey
often grow enormous leaves,
making the best use of the limited
light available.

Flower Inflorescence
(Calathea sp.)
An inflorescence is a collection of
flowers on the same stem. On this
plant, the flowers come out, one by
one, over a period of about a
month.

Bromeliad
(Billbergia zebrina)
A mass of brightly-coloured
flowers, which burst into bloom
within days of each other, attracts
hummingbirds to collect the
nectar.

RIGHT:
Bromeliad
(Neoregelia sp.)
The way in which colour intensifies
towards the centre of this plant
serves to guide nectar gatherers to
the food source.

Colour

The smooth tones and patterns of a butterfly's wing reveal
overlapping scales of pigment when viewed in close-up,
which combine to reflect light in a pattern to confuse or to
attract. The bright plumage of hummingbirds is made, not
from pigments, but from minute patterns in the wing surface
which scatter light into different colours. Colours are used
both to repel and to attract, and are vital to many animals in
the forest. How the eye-spot patterns on insect wings could
have evolved even to include reflected highlights in the
'pupils' baffles the imagination and indicates the stunning
powers of natural selection in this diverse world which we
are only just beginning to understand. One does not have to
be a biologist to enjoy the sheer beauty of this enchanting
place or to recognize the extent to which our world would
become impoverished should such natural treasures be
allowed to vanish forever. Few people have the opportunity
to visit all the great art collections of the world, but surely
even fewer would be willing to see them burnt to the ground?
No artist could have fashioned such patterns, each of which
lends to an animal or plant a special advantage, but which
can also bring such delight to the human spirit.

Green-Winged Macaw
(Ara chloroptera)
Wing and (left) eye

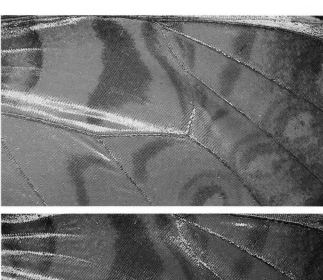

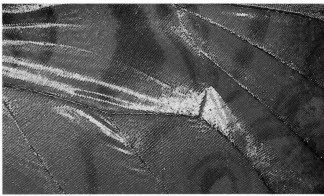

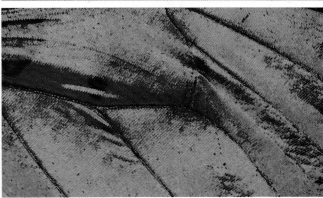

Morpho Butterfly
(Morpho sulkowski)
Wing of the male morpho butterfly. Some of the most brilliant colours in nature, particularly those found in the tropics, are not produced by pigments but by diffraction. Here, the finely spaced surface structure of the macaw's feathers and the morpho butterfly's wing scales breaks up white light reflected onto it into its component spectral colours. In the case of the morpho, an electric blue is reflected, while the rest of the spectrum is scattered. The camouflaged underside of its wing shows through as brown. As these huge butterflies flit through the dappled light of the forest, their wings flash blue as they appear and disappear with each wingbeat. The males have definite flight paths through the forest, located between thirty and forty metres (90–120 feet) above ground level.

Swallow Tanager
(Tersina viridis)
The female bird shown here is camouflaged with green plumage so that she can rear her young undetected. The mating ritual of swallow tanagers involves an extraordinary gathering of flocks during which males and females stretch and bow to one another amid much squawking.

Black-Headed Squirrel Monkey
(Saimiri sp.)
This small monkey's extreme agility helps it to escape from its principal predator, the harpy eagle. It lives in family groups and eats fruit, insects and young leaves.

RIGHT:
Forest Squirrel
(Sciurus sp.)

OPPOSITE:
White-Tailed Deer
(Odocoileus sp.)
This secretive and timorous vegetarian lives only in pristine forest where there are no humans. One of its few predators is the jaguar.

Owl Monkey
(Aotus trivirgatus)
Like its namesake, the owl monkey is nocturnal, relying on its large, sensitive eyes to see in the very dimmest light. Owl monkeys are monogamous and wander around the forest in small groups.

OPPOSITE:
Cotton-Topped Tamarin
(Saguinus oedipus)
The tamarin is one of the closest relatives to man. It lives in trees where it eats bugs, insects, lizards, frogs, nectar and tree gum. Its claw-like nails are used for gripping tree bark. The cotton-topped tamarin comes from North Colombia.

Bushmaster Snake
(Lachesis muta)
This large and extremely
venomous viper lies curled on the
forest floor, perfectly camouflaged
amongst the leaf-litter, waiting
motionless for some hapless rodent
or other small animal to pass by.

RIGHT:
Leaf-Cutter Ant
(Atta cephalotes)
The parasol or leaf-cutting ant
climbs high into trees to cut
portions of leaves which it carries
away to its nest underground.
Often long files of laden workers
can be seen. The ants do not feed
on the leaves but use them as a
medium on which to grow fungi
which they then eat. This ant is
carrying calliandra florets.

Army Ants
(Eciton sp.)
Here, tens of thousands of army
ants have massed to create a forty-
five-centimetre (eighteen-inch)
bivouac on a hollow tree. This will
be the nest for reproduction,
hatching and food collection. The
worker ants hang in a network,
connected by their legs and jaws,
and protect the larvae, the pupae
and the queen in the very centre of
this structure.

Netted-Winged Homopteran
(Pterygota sp.)
This homopteran is unusual in
having wings which are angled
outwards from its body when
closed, rather than fitting tightly
along its back. Like its entire family
it is a sap-sucker.

Millepede
Rolled up in a defensive posture,
this millepede strongly resembles a
fossilized ammonite.

Form

The dwarfs and giants which exist in rainforests make them
compelling places to explore. There are butterflies with
wings the size of a human hand, hummingbirds as small as
bumblebees, bird-eating spiders, snails larger than duck eggs,
millepedes twenty-five centimetres (ten inches) long, and
violets the size of apple trees. All insects have six legs, a
thorax and an abdomen but they can be disguised in many
ways. Some look like leaves with limbs, others have wings so
clear that they are almost invisible. Still others disguise
themselves as water droplets or bird droppings, or decorate
their bodies with faecal matter to look like mould – the aim is
to resemble anything but a meal. A close-up view of a beetle's
face reveals a design of devastating efficiency: large
compound eyes, crucial for detecting minute movements in
the forest, each lens creating a small view of the world, and
immensely sharp jaws made of chitin for crunching through
other insect bodies or for eating hardwood. Here, nature
produces architecture and graphic design of unimaginable
variety.

Harlequin Beetle
(Acrocinus longimanus)
Up to twenty-five centimetres (ten inches) in length, this huge beetle has the capacity to inflict a painful bite with its mandibles. It also emits a loud rasping sound when upset.

False Coral Snake
(Oxyrhopus sp.)
The warning coloration of the false coral snake echoes that of the exceedingly venomous true coral snake; both use it to gain protection from their enemies.

Common Iguana
(Iguana iguana)
The iguana is a tree-dweller and climbs efficiently with the help of extremely sharp claws. Just like some dinosaurs, it has small plates set upright along its spine which, recent theories argue, may act as cooling surfaces (centre right). It has no outer ear, and its ear-drum (far right above) is set flush with its metallically shaded scales (far right below).

Common American Anole
Unlike the iguana, which appears inactive, this anole scampers around the canopy at high speed and with great agility. Like the chameleon, it is capable of changing colour to merge in with its background.

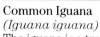

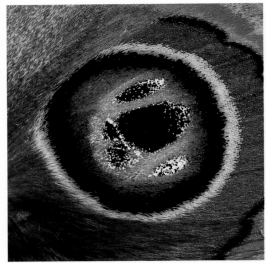

ABOVE:
Wing of the Hairstreak Butterfly
(Thecla coronata)

TOP:
Eyespot on the wing of a Silkmoth
(Lancanella contempta)

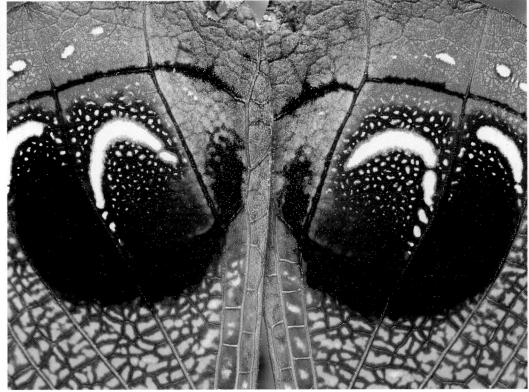

ABOVE:
Eyespots of a False Leaf Katydid

TOP:
Forest Crab
The forest crab can wander a long
way from water to scavenge on the
forest floor. Its gill chambers are
modified with spongy tissue,
enabling the creature to respire in
air.

Army Ants
(Eciton sp.)
Contravening all the normal rules
of ant behaviour, army ants do not
have a permanent home, but
wander around, gypsy-like,
occupying temporary bivouacs.
They are savage predators,
aggressively attacking any form of
animal life in the path of the
hunting column.

Ant Scavengers

Ants are great scavengers and are some of the most resilient
creatures in the forest. There are many types. Some, less than
two millimetres long, search for the minute seeds of *miconia*
plants. These seeds, smaller than a pin-head, are removed
from the droppings of birds. Tiny starchy appendages on the
seeds may be used by the ants for food. By dispersing them,
these small ants play a vital role in the spread of *miconia*
seeds to germination sites. The *iridomyrmex* ants scavenge
the forest floor for the carcasses of dead insects. They gather
these into their arboreal nests which rest inside the football-
sized epiphytic plants found growing on tree branches. The
ants feed on the fungi which grows on the insect remains
stored inside their plant homes. Most impressive of all are the
army ants which patrol the forest floor in huge columns, the
workers protected by enormous soldiers, each capable of
inflicting a painful bite. Any beetle, caterpillar or millepede,
in fact almost anything they can overpower, is dismembered
to provide food for their larvae protected inside the army
ants' bivouac.

3
Communication

The forest is a noisy place in which to make oneself heard. Millions of insects buzz, scrape and stridulate, producing a multitude of different calls which vie for attention in a constant hiss of sound. From the bright canopy to the mottled understorey numerous creeping things face the dilemma of making themselves noticeable to friends while remaining unnoticed by enemies. The first is essential for successful sex, the second necessary to avoid being eaten. The result is confusing for human senses, even though our nostrils, eyes and ears are too feeble to catch most of the sensory signals which fill the forest.

To stay in touch in a rainforest you must either be very noisy, very colourful, or very smelly. In all the great rainforests of the world there are monkeys with loud voices. The most tuneful are the gibbons of the Asian forests, but none are louder than the howlers of Central and South America. Their penetrating roars alert other groups to their position so that all utilize the forest whilst minimizing combat over resources. Most monkeys and apes call just before dawn as sound travels further in the cool air above the canopy; and later on the cacophony of insect and bird noise might drown them out. Many birds in the high canopy have twittering calls which convey a variety of information, but which would be absorbed and silenced by the thick vegetation below, so birds that live in the understorey have simple repetitive songs or deep booming calls that carry well through the dense foliage. The cicada is the loudest insect in the forest and is also one of the oldest. Cicadas may spend thirteen years as larvae beneath the soil before metamorphosing into winged adults which fill the trees with sound.

With a pervading background of green it is not surprising that plants and animals often use the complementary colour, red, to attract attention. The starburst cluster of red *Brownea rose-de-monte* flowers attracts the hummingbirds whose beaks are designed to probe the flower tubes for nectar. Many birds are especially sensitive to red and trees clothe their crowns in red flowers in order to attract them. When ripe, fruits are also advertised in the same way to attract birds to eat them. Sometimes the bright colour is hidden beneath a green case which has a brilliant red aril coating beneath. Only when the seed is ready for transport to a germination site does the case split open, the red interior signalling a feast to passing birds. Flowers designed to attract insects may be coloured in yellows or violets, but may also contain hidden ultra-violet colours, visible only to insects which use them as nectar guides. Many butterflies with iridescent blue wings, such as morphos, are also patterned in ultra-violet, which flashes brilliantly in colours we cannot see but which might attract a mate.

While some birds are cryptically coloured and go unnoticed, many use breathtaking combinations of blues, reds, greens and yellows to advertise their presence and to repel. The green plumage of quetzals and trogons serves as camouflage, and startling flashes of the red feathers between wing and breast confuse predators.

Colour combined with movement is a powerful flag. A toucan's beak is more than a tool for plucking fruit. It enables teams of these colourful birds to stay in touch. One frog may wave a coloured leg to another in amphibian semaphore if the waterfall they are sitting by is too loud for their calls to be heard.

The rich scents of the forest are unforgettable. During the day the fine smells of orchids float down from the canopy mixed with those of a thousand flowers from gigantic tree crowns whose florets and petals have fallen to the forest floor. The purpose of these messages is to attract nectar-feeding birds and insects who will carry pollen from flower to flower. By night the forest is filled with the heavy perfume of moth- and bat-pollenated flowers which are often coloured white to make them easy to find in the moonlight.

Our noses are too weak to smell the forest's most potent odours, those of territorial markers positioned by mammals on branches or leaves, and are still less able to detect the most far-reaching of all odours, insect pheromones. From a perch in the canopy a female butterfly may distribute perfumes on the wind from her exposed pencil hairs, and a male may detect them more than two kilometres away. Using his highly sensitive antennae, he will fly unerringly towards the source with the tenacity of an entomological bloodhound. Occasionally a tall shrub may be lit up at night like a Christmas tree, with tiny flashing white lights, as fireflies dance a mating ritual thousands of years old. Different species have evolved their own code to avoid confusion and still more clever is the spider that mimics them and attracts the fireflies to his larder.

PREVIOUS PAGE:
Morpho Butterfly
(Morpho sulkowski)
This is the epitome of a showy South American butterfly. Hand-sized, its flashing iridescent blue wings distinguish it from all others. It manages to elude most predators by means of its fast, erratic flight, although the persistent naturalist can usually catch one by waiting by one of its regular flight paths with a net.

Postman Butterfly
(Heliconius melpomene)
This group of butterflies contains some of the most beautiful in the New World, and is also famous for the number of its members who mimic other groups. Moreover, the postman butterfly has so many different colour forms that one could look at a dozen or more and be forgiven for thinking that they all belonged to totally different species.

OPPOSITE:
Wild Silkmoth
(Automeris sp.*)*
When at rest amongst leaf-litter, the wild silkmoth is perfectly camouflaged by its leaf-like coloration. However, should a bird or lizard investigate it, the moth springs its front wings forward to reveal the eyespots on its rear wings. A similar trick is worked by some frogs who have the same sort of marks on their hind legs.

Warning Signs

Many butterflies, moths and bugs camouflage themselves on one side of their wings, allowing their bodies to vanish into the forest background. If discovered by a prying bird or lizard they sweep their wings apart to reveal menacing eyes and bright patterns, sufficiently startling the aggressor, if only for a moment, to allow them to make their escape. A silk moth may have three lines of defence: camouflage, a startle display, and flight. Surprise is the key factor in the success of a startle display. The cigar-sized caterpillars of certain sphinx moths, if disturbed, rear up and inflate their bodies, imitating the shape and markings of a viper. Some warning colours are almost universal. The yellow and black of hornets and wasps are a popular combination, used to advertise danger. Deadly coral snakes are coloured red and yellow, yet some edible snakes emulate this colouring and benefit from the deception. Such duplicity also occurs in unrelated butterflies whose striking red-and-black or yellow-and-black patterns indicate unpalatability, though many of them are in fact edible. For such a deception to work the models must always outnumber the mimics, or random selection will favour the predator taking a chance on an appetizing victim.

Poison-Dart Frogs
(Dendrobates pumilio)
Two male poison frogs are fighting over a particularly choice territory. In a prolonged brawl, they wrestle and tumble over among the leaf-litter until one of them gives up the fight and quickly hops away. These frogs produce one of the most poisonous vertebrate venoms, dendrobatin, in their mucus. The substance is used by Amazonian Indians to prime their hunting darts, hence the name.

Staking a Claim

Howler monkeys howl, frogs peep, and cats spray bushes, all to protect the territory which provides food for them and their families whilst avoiding combat. When a frog calls in the darkness, a butterfly dances in a shaft of sunlight, or a male monkey hoots through the dawn or dusk, are these animal prospectors attracting mates or repelling interlopers? Often they are doing both. Many nocturnally calling frogs have two components to their calls. The male *coqui* frog of Puerto Rico begins his evening by marching to a favoured leaf and sets up a territory with a repeated 'ko' call. If another male ventures too close, an amphibian wrestling match breaks out until one retires. When the male has established his territory, he changes his tune and adds a 'kee' note, singing 'ko-kee'. Hearing that the fighting is over, the females move in to choose their mate.

To avoid competition and conflict most animals will threaten one another. Pioneering humans, however, are no respecters of territory in the rainforest, and the Indians there have had to resort to fighting to protect what they know to be theirs. They are gradually gaining a stronger voice as the outside world learns of their plight, and the cry for their survival grows louder every day.

Gecko
(Gonatodes ceciliae)
To display his stake on territory
and to ward off potential invaders,
this male gecko is stretching to full
height and curling his tail for added
effect. The female of the species
has subtle, olive-brown colouring
and is attracted by the gaudy
costume of the male.

Red Howler Monkey
(Alouatta senicula)
With its weird, leopard-like cry, this
monkey can be heard up to eight
kilometres (five miles) away.
Territory is defined by this howling.
Here, it displays the fact that it is
the dominant male. Red howler
monkeys live in family groups
made up of one male and several
females: as soon as other, younger
males reach maturity they are sent
away to fend for themselves.

Cicada
(Family Cicadidae)
The male cicada's stridulating organs – small drums set in the side of its body – enable it to produce a high-pitched pulsating din to attract females. As adults, these canopy-dwelling sap-suckers have a brief life, but the nymphs of many species may spend some years underground, feeding on the roots of plants.

Poison-Dart Frog
(Dendrobates pumilio)
Males adopt a proud, bull-dog posture like this and make a peeping noise to attract potential mates. Warning coloration works to deter possible predators, such as lizards, snakes, crabs or birds, even when the frogs are in exposed places.

A Symphony of Sound

Nightfall is one of the most enchanting times in the forest. As blood-red skies darken to blue, the nocturnal creatures begin to call in symphony. The birds of the day sing their last song and cicadas punctuate the dusk with penetratingly individual sounds, signing off their territories before the long night shift begins. It is at this time that the frogs come into their own. Each species has its own call. Some croak from beneath leaves, others pipe beside stones, still more 'dink' furiously from high in the canopy. The forest tune changes as the evening wears on, with early callers retiring and new ones taking their places. Eventually the forest chorus line settles into a pulsating rhythm that lasts throughout the night and gradually fades as dawn approaches. Then the cicadas begin again, like a myriad tiny chain saws, piercing the awakening forest. The males click a small convex plate in the skin on each side of the abdomen at a rate of more than a thousand times per second, all the time watching for an approaching female signalling acceptance with a flicker of her wings.

Grasshopper
(Taeniopoda sp.)
The eardrums of this grasshopper
are located on the sides of its body.
Its sense of hearing is vital for
survival, not only to warn of danger
but also to pick up the signals of
courtship. Since hearing is more
important at night than during the
day, it is more acute in nocturnal
creatures.

Red-Eyed Tree Frog
(Agalychnis callidryas)
The red-eyed tree frog is one of the
most appealing of amphibians. This
one is emerging from its day-time
hideaway in a bromeliad.

Ithomid Butterfly
(Sais sp.)
These butterflies are Müellerian mimics and use shallow wing-beats to best show off their distinctive wing patterns. Müellerian mimicry describes the way in which such poisonous insects have evolved to resemble one another and give the same signals of distastefulness to would-be predators.

Ithomid Butterfly
(Sais sp.*)*
Together with the Heliconids, the Ithomid butterflies shown here are amongst the most vivid and attractive inhabitants of the South American rainforest. They may be seen darting about whenever one comes across a small patch of sunlight breaking through the canopy.

Skeleton Butterfly
(Pteronymia sp.*)*

Pierid Butterfly

(Family Pieridae)

From the same family as the Cabbage White, this butterfly is a Müellerian mimic. Its red and yellow colours, set off against a black background, show potential predators that it will be distasteful. Unusually for a butterfly, though common amongst moths, this species has the habit of shivering to bring its wing muscles up to the temperature required for flight.

ABOVE:
That it shows itself off so openly is evidence of its invulnerability.

Day-Flying Moth
(Mesonthen petosiris)
Here is another mimic: a moth that looks and even sounds like a wasp. When an animal pretends to have the characteristics of something unpleasant in order to protect itself, it is known as a Batesian mimic, after the nineteenth-century English naturalist Henry Walter Bates who first described the deception.

Poison-Dart Frog
(Dendrobates pumilio)
Thanks to their warning coloration, these notoriously poisonous frogs can move around the forest in the middle of the day without any risk of being attacked.

The male of the species carries the tadpoles around on his back, transporting them between one pool and another, and occasionally into bromeliads high above the forest floor.

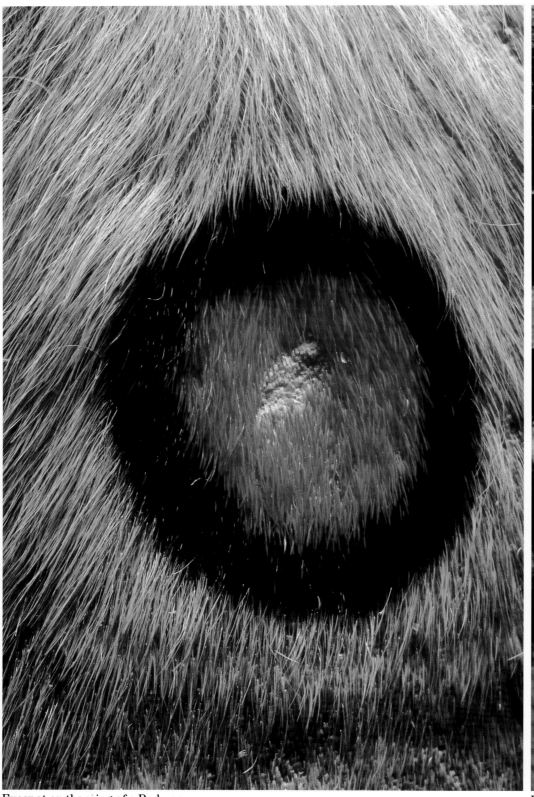

Eyespot on the wing of a Redmoon Silkmoth
(Gamelia rubriluna)
Detail of the topside hind wing.

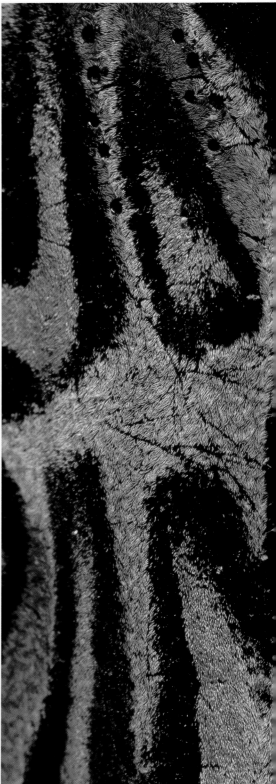

Elytra of the Harlequin Beetle
(Acrocinus longimanus)
Elytra are the hard covers that protect the beetle's delicate wings when it is at rest. In flight they act as fixed aerofoils while the wings flap behind.

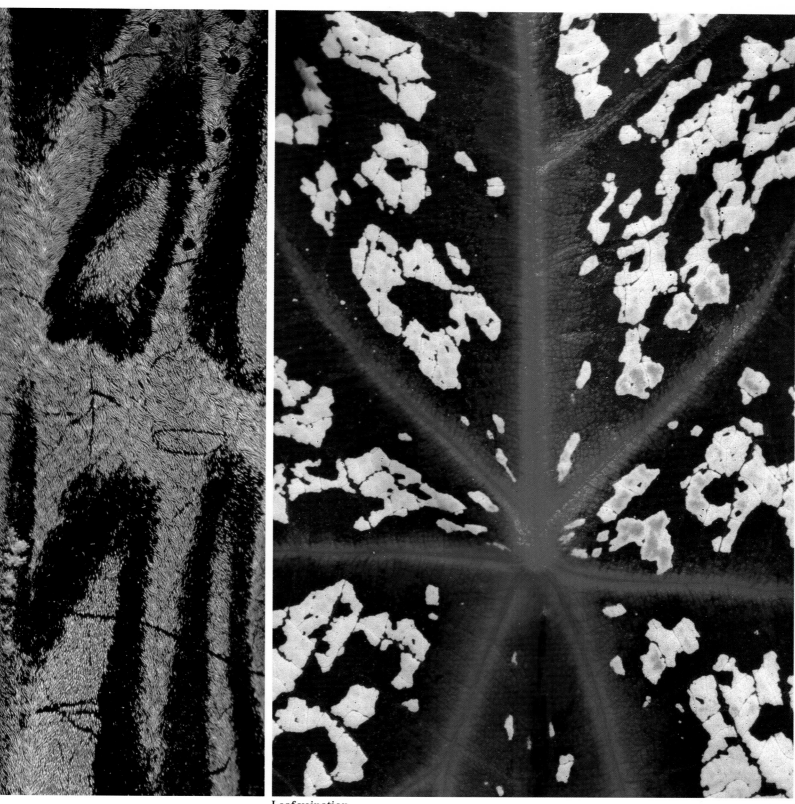

Leaf veination
(Caladio bicolor)
Close-up of the bright-red
veination of a typical rainforest
leaf.

Pyralid Moth
(Diaphania sp.*)*
During its mating period, this moth puts out pencil hairs from its abdomen to waft sexually attractive pheromones on the breeze, creating a scent trail to enable potential mates to fly towards the source. When not in use, these hairs retract into the body.

Potent Perfumes

Smells are a vital method of communication for numerous creatures in the forest. Some monkeys have chest glands with which they rub signals on tree bark, marmosets rub their genitals on branches, bushbabies urinate onto their feet, dabbing territorial markers with each step. Peccaries, the pigs of the South American rainforest, mark their territories on rocks and tree trunks with secretions from a rump gland and use dung piles to define core areas. A gland below their eyes distributes a cohesive group smell when individuals from the same herd rub faces, rather as the domestic cat rubs its face against us with apparent affection. None of these means are as effective as the pheromones deployed by insects. Pheromones are the most potent attractants known in the world and can be detected by male butterflies and moths in concentrations of just a few molecules over distances of up to two kilometres. They are produced in special glands in the abdomen of the insect and are then coated onto special 'hair pencils' which are waved in the breeze.

Moth
(Mapeta xanthomelas)
Warningly coloured, the yellow on
this moth shows that it will smell
and taste bad. It was first
discovered in Venezuela by a pet
capuchine monkey belonging to
William Beebe, the founder of the
Tropical Department of the New
York Zoological Society.

4
Movement

Rainforests are often thought of as impenetrable. No vehicle has been designed to travel through them rapidly, and they remain the least-explored environment on earth. Once inside a forest it is easy to get lost. All the trees look the same and there are no clues to help with orientation. Hooked vines cling to clothes, and some trees tower seventy metres (200 feet) high on smooth trunks, while others are coated with vines and ferns in which poisonous snakes and stinging insects may lurk. High above, a maze of branches fills the sky.

On the ground, water is often a barrier to movement in the forest. When the Amazon floods, land animals must escape to higher ground, take to the trees or literally walk on water. None is more adept at the latter than the Jesus Christ lizard which flails its feet on the water surface at such speed that it can cross streams and rivers easily. The largest snake in the world, the anaconda, often hunts its prey in water, as do the alligators and crocodiles that share the forest floor with non-climbing animals such as giant anteaters, pigs and tapirs.

Trunks and branches offer alternative paths. Far from being the confusing maze it appears to us, the canopy is, to the animals that live there, a collection of favourite walks. Its limbs, vines, columns and tendrils are in fact a network of carefully memorized arboreal highways used by spider monkeys, squirrels, lizards, mice and rats. Leaf-cutting ants have their own miniature routes leading from the canopy, where they cut choice leaves, all the way down to their nests under the ground. Branches regularly used as animal trails are carpeted with moss, a gallery of ferns and other epiphytes on either side.

Most arboreal animals have evolved powerful hands, feet and claws to let them clamber sedately through the branches. Tree frogs have developed pads of adhesive hairs on their toes to enable themselves to cling to leaves, but they rarely leap. Some flatten their bellies to the underside of leaf surfaces, using suction to secure their position while at rest. Snakes are ideally suited to a forest environment. Many are exquisitely camouflaged and their sinewy, muscular bodies enable them to slide through the branches in search of nests of young birds. The blunt-headed tree snake has a remarkable backbone which enables it to stretch, rigidly supported, across gaps in the foliage in its search for sleeping lizards amongst the leaves.

New World monkeys have powerful jumping legs and also prehensile tails which they use to anchor themselves, freeing their hands to grasp foods that other less well-equipped creatures cannot reach. The flying monkeys or sakis of Colombia are capable of prodigious leaps through the trees. They gallop along tree boughs leaping as far as thirty metres (three hundred feet) through the air to another tree. Their diet is of unripe seeds that are too poisonous for other monkeys and they must cover large areas of forest to find enough of them. In complete contrast, sloths never need to travel far to find food because they eat simply leaves. However, leaves are not very nutritious so sloths must conserve energy. They move only at a glacial pace, and remain immobile for much of the day, hanging under branches with their special locking claws.

As the crowns of the forest trees rarely interlock, animals travelling between them must be capable of leaping, gliding or flying. The region of columns beneath the canopy is used by animals with powerful back legs, known as clingers and leapers, such as the lemurs in Madagascar, tarsiers in Asia and marmosets in South America. These latter creatures gnaw the bark of tree trunks to obtain sap and gum and gather insects from the branches. In order to lengthen the distance they can jump, many animals have evolved parachutes of skin – examples include gliding squirrels, gliding frogs and even gliding snakes.

Peering into the forest, it is easy to see that it is composed of corridors and tunnels used as flyways by insects, birds and bats. Eagles and hawks which hunt in the forest have short stubby wings designed for rapid direction changes. Hummingbirds may beat their wings a hundred times a second and can hover precisely in front of flowers or pluck tiny insects from the air. Parrots dive through the canopy with breath-taking speed, while insectivorous birds flow through the forest in a mixed feeding flock. Butterflies as large as a human hand float on warm air currents in these corridors, dwarfing the gnats that revolve like dust particles in shafts of sunlight. To the smallest insects the humid air is something almost to swim through. Many more insects fly at night, when the humidity is higher than by day.

Insectivorous bats can see, but use sonar to find their way around at night. They have sophisticated sonic radar and navigate through dense branches with dazzling ease. The speed and location of their prey is deduced by the returning echo which changes tune in the same way as the sound of a horn alters as a car rushes past a bystander. After dark, bats hunting at different heights fill the forest with twitters and clicks. Numerous insects take to the air during rain, either because they have been dislodged from leaves or knowing that the bats' radar cannot distinguish them from water droplets.

Hawk Moths in flight
(Family Sphingidae)
These robust, high-speed moths hover like hummingbirds and pollinate flowers at night with tongues that coil up like watchsprings and then unfurl to suck in nectar. Night-flying insects are most abundant on misty, moonless nights, yet despite the seemingly impossible conditions for high-speed flying they avoid crashing into obstacles. During the daytime they are found at rest on tree trunks and branches everywhere, from the forest floor to the canopy. They are a popular food source for birds, squirrels and possums.

PREVIOUS PAGE:

Basilisk or **Jesus Lizard**
(Basiliscus plumifrons)
There can be few sights in the forest more astonishing than that of a large lizard running across the surface of a pond or pool. To avoid predators, the basilisk has developed the extraordinary ability to run over water without sinking. As the creature does not have webbed feet, how it achieves this is unclear – perhaps its sheer speed keeps it afloat. The tail is used to aid balance, rather like that of a kangaroo.

The overall effect of the canopy is that of a crazy mosaic of light and dark. As the word suggests, the canopy is a high network of pathways and feeding stations for its inhabitants.

Cheating Death

Walking beneath the forest canopy by day or night the forest-watcher has little idea of the trials of strength that are progressing high above his or her head. It takes a special patience even to observe the infinitely complex ways of the forest and its inhabitants. How long must it take to unravel the mysteries of the superb sonic radar of a massive bat which cruises the high canopy snatching moths in total darkness? Moths, too, have ears and can hear the bats coming. If our ears were as sensitive as those of many moths, the forest at night would sound like a room filled with babbling children. The problem for the moth is to pick out the sound which spells death whilst also concentrating on its next meal and the tantalizing prospect of a mate. Tiger moths taste unpleasant and are brightly coloured to warn of this, but their livery is useless at night when it is too dark to see them. They rely instead on last-minute avoiding action as the bat is on its final approach, and if this fails can produce a series of loud clicks similar to those of the bat's own sonar. Disorientated, the bat may miss the moth and fly off in search of easier prey.

Epiphyte on a palm stilt
(*Ireartea gigantea*)

Reaching for the Light

Some seeds remain dormant for years before a tree falls and a gap appears in the forest roof. The increase in soil temperature triggers a race to the canopy. Whilst pioneer species such as *cercropia* and balsa trees are sprinters and quickly fill the gap, their lives are short, leaving canopy marathon runners such as mahogany to take their place. All of these must run the gauntlet of lianas, vines and other clinging plants which, having no stout trunks of their own, attach themselves to tree bark in order to gain a place in the sun.

OPPOSITE:
Common Iguana
(*Iguana iguana*)
A common iguana in the sub-canopy, about thirty to forty metres (100 to 130 feet) above the ground. Iguanas can measure up to two metres (six-and-a-half feet) long, including their tails. Long claws and digits make them agile climbers and they will also readily take to water if alarmed. They lay their eggs on the forest floor: on hatching out, the young climb up into the trees. At night they return to roost in a bed of leaves. Iguanas will eat insects but are largely vegetarian.

OVERLEAF:
Lianas
Much of the character of the forest is provided by these remarkable plants. They cling to trees and grow with them into the canopy. When their host tree falls, they may climb another, so reaching a great age and size. They are shown here festooning a large tree.

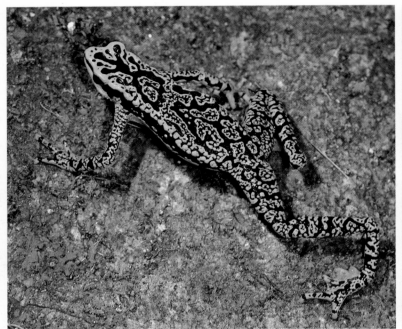

Green Mosaic Frog
(Atelopus crucigas)
The yellow-and-black coloration of
this frog advertises its poisonous
toxins so that predators learn to
avoid it.

Alligator Lizard
(Gerrhonotus sp.*)*
About twenty-five centimetres (ten
inches) in length, this sub-canopy
lizard has a prehensile tail with
which it can attach itself to
branches.

OPPOSITE:
Stilt Palm
(Socratea durissima)
This tree's trunk is very short and
is supported by small aerated roots
which grow downwards into the
earth. These palms are common in
parts of the forest susceptible to
flooding.

OVERLEAF, LEFT:
**Green-Cheeked Amazon
Hummingbird**
(Amazonia vevecligenalis)

OVERLEAF, RIGHT:
Orange-Winged Amazon Parrot
(Amazonia amazonica)
Parrots are highly intelligent and
gregarious birds, and the tropical
forests in which they spend their
lives are brightened by their gay
colours and resound with their
chattering and shrieking calls.

Walking the
Twilight Zone

Some tidy-minded biologists have perpetrated the myth that
the rainforest is divided into neat layers, like a cake. The
reality is much more complex. Trees of all shapes and heights
intermingle and beneath them are shrubs and palms specially
adapted to living in the twilight zone. It is only when climbing
up a rope from the floor of the forest to the canopy that a real
appreciation of the corridors and rooms of the rainforest
apartment block is possible. There is no obvious layering, but
certain species will never grow to be canopy giants while
other trees will in time spread their crowns above the forest
roof as emergents. Another myth is that the jungle is
impenetrable. On the edges of rivers and clearings it appears
so because of the tangles of vines, palms and shrubs which
scramble for light at these forest boundaries. A pristine forest
which has matured over hundreds of years is as open inside
as a beechwood. If one follows an animal trail, and takes care
not to trip over a trailing liana or a buttress root, it is a
pleasant place for a stroll.

Praying Mantis
(Acanthops fulcatus)
This wolf in sheep's clothing preys on smaller insects that come within its range as it wanders through the leaf-litter. However, if molested by a creature bigger than itself, it falls over and pretends to be dead. Its brown, leaf-like appearance helps its defence.

Katydid
(Family Pseudophyllidae)
The name of the family means 'false leaf' and the wings of this katydid look like dead leaves. If disturbed, it raises its front wings violently and reveals its back wings and their eyespots, whose small, white crescent-shaped markings give the impression of highlights in mammalian eyes.

Hairstreak Butterfly
(Family Lycaenidae)
The males rub their back wings together and release scent scales to attract females. Some biologists believe that the patterned end of the wings and the white-tipped hairs are designed to encourage predators to that part of the butterfly, rather than to its head which would be a more disastrous loss.

Three-Toed Sloth
(Bradypus variegatus)
A sloth on one of its rare journeys to the ground. Its musty-smelling fur is cultured with algae, giving it a greenish colour which provides useful camouflage from harpy eagles. When it is curled up asleep, the sloth looks remarkably like a termite's nest. Its fur also houses beetles, and moths which lay their eggs in its faeces.

A slow-moving forest stream.

OPPOSITE:
Red-Eyed Tree Frog
(Agalychnis callidryas)
After waking from its daytime
roost, lying flat and well
camouflaged on a green leaf, the
frog's search for food begins.
Before leaping it gauges the
position of its prey or intended
landing point, then launches itself
into the air with its powerful hind
legs. The eyes are contracted into
the sockets during the jump.

ABOVE LEFT:
Baird's Tapir
(Tapirus bairdii)
Measuring about two metres (six-and-a-half feet) in length, this animal is the largest herbivore in the forest. Apart from man its only real enemies are the jaguar and the caiman. Tapirs are agile swimmers and are mainly nocturnal.

Lit by a beam of sunlight, epiphytes grow on a fallen branch submerged in a stream.

Fishing Bat
(Noctilio sp.*)*
Like many species of bat, the
fishing bat possesses a complex
sonic radar, enabling it to 'hear' the
size, shape, texture and distance of
objects around. It is able to locate
fish acoustically by sensing the
ripples produced by a fish on the
water's surface.

5
Finding Food

Numerous foods from rainforests, such as brazil nuts, avocados, figs, even coffee and cocoa, now find their way to our tables, but few of us give a second thought as to where they came from, or why the brazil nut is so hard or the avocado so rich. The rainforest is like an enormous supermarket in which the packaging is often highly coloured but the labelling is in unreadable hieroglyphics. Only local Indians and the creatures of the forest can recognize the products. Their skills are vital because, far from being edible, many fruits of the forest are filled with deadly poisons.

Through millenniums a battle has raged amongst the trees and the smaller plants of the forest to defend their fruits and leaves against hungry marauders. In order to capture the energy of the sun a tree must produce new leaves, each of which is a potential meal to a passing monkey, leaf-cutting ant or caterpillar. Unpalatability through chemical weapons is often the major line of defence. In response, caterpillars tend to become specialized in attacking a single species with whose poisons they can cope. The poisons of highly toxic plants such as passion flower vines are often turned to advantage and are stored or even synthesized by insects for their own protection. A caterpillar filled with plant poison advertises the fact with bright colours and patterns so that its predators will learn to avoid it.

Many insects can only attack young leaves which have yet to become toughened or toxic. Lines of holes in old leaves have often been formed by an insect burrowing through the furled leaf when it was young. Leaf-cutting ants harvest mature leaves but do not actually eat them. Instead, they carry choice green crescents of leaf in their jaws from the canopy into their underground nests, where they 'seed' them with fungal spores. The fungi break down the tough leaf material and thrive on the nutrients released, and the ants eat their tiny sporing mushrooms.

To survive on indigestible leaves requires a lengthy gut full of bacteria. A large bellyful of gently composting leaves is no asset to agile monkeys or flying birds, so there are few groups of grazers in the canopy, and no birds which exist on leaves alone, despite the abundance of this low energy source. Although the sloth and the iguana exploit this niche, climbing ponderously through the branches, the former must remain slothful or run out of energy, and the latter needs to warm itself in the canopy's sun or suffer the same fate.

Many trees need to attract animals to eat their fruits and drop the seeds, so dispersing the offspring they contain. Such a dangerous solution must also defend itself against seed predators such as parrots, weevils and peccaries who eat the seeds and destroy them. The brazil-nut tree conceals the nuts inside a cannon-ball-sized pod which, when ripe, ejects them to the ground. The nuts are themselves exceptionally difficult to break into in order to protect them from rodents and weevils on the forest floor. Only the agouti's teeth are strong enough to destroy the seeds, but its habit of burying large numbers of them as a food store ensures that some are forgotten and will germinate.

Large, rich seeds, such as avocados, contain an almost complete diet of proteins and fats for the animals which rely on them for food. Many animals and birds which eat such seeds, among them quetzals, are specialists and consume little else. On being swallowed, the fruit's rich flesh is digested off. The seed itself is strongly protected and is eventually either regurgitated or passes through the digestive system unscathed. In this way trees have evolved a partnership of mutual dependence with a specific disperser. Trees such as figs employ an entirely different strategy. They produce vast numbers of small seeds embedded in a colourful, fleshy fruit which is very palatable. Pigeons, spider monkeys, toucans and bats crowd around these trees picking a bountiful harvest. It is no accident that syrup of figs is a laxative. The fig trees evolved it that way. Most of the seeds pass through the guts of these creatures rapidly, and though many may be ground up in the pigeon's gizzard, the sheer number of them ensures that some will pass through unharmed.

In Africa, the seeds of *Panda oleosa* will germinate only once they have passed through an elephant, and have been given a good start by using the elephant's dung as a nutrient supply. Some huge seeds which now fall to the ground in Central American rainforests may originally have evolved to be eaten and dispersed by mastodons, large, elephant-like creatures, which used to roam the forests there. The tough seeds of the *Calvaria* tree in Mauritius may once have been dispersed by the extinct dodo. In modern times, *Calvaria* seeds first germinated when they were fed to imported turkeys. These stories illustrate the interdependence of the forest and its animals. The giant trees of the canopy may depend for their survival on a single bat or bird which is the means of dispersal of their offspring.

Leaf-Cutter Ant
(Atta cephalotes)
This ant is cutting a circular piece of *Banisteriopsis caapi* leaf with its jaw. When the circle has been cut out, it will be carried back to the nest and chewed up into a mulch. A fungus grows on it, the fruiting bodies of which provide food for the ant. This type of leaf is made into snuff by Amazon Indians and is used in tribal rituals.

PREVIOUS PAGE:
Oasis Hummingbird
(Family Trochilidae)
The hummingbird is found only in the New World, from the Amazon to the High Andes. Although mainly a nectar feeder, it does supplement its diet with insects caught in flight. Hummingbirds are highly territorial, swooping and chattering aggressively at any intruder which dares to invade their area, and readily taking on birds much larger than themselves.

Blood-Eared Parrakeet
(Pyrrhura hoematotis)
This parrakeet is mashing up an unripe canopy fruit before eating it. All the parrot family are highly developed for a life in the trees, using both beaks and feet to climb in the canopy. Their feet are also efficient in shelling and stoning fruit and seeds; the powerful beaks of birds such as this tend to destroy seeds rather than dispersing them.

BELOW:
White-Necked Jacobin Hummingbird
(Florisuga mellivora)
The white-necked Jacobin is one of the most common and widespread species of hummingbird, noted by many of the early explorers to South America. Here, a palm leaf has provided an ideal nesting site.

OPPOSITE:
Salvin's Amazon Parrot
(Amazona autumnalis salvini)
The red fruit on which this attractive parrot is feeding is known locally as the wild cherry. Salvin's Amazon inhabits Central America and the northern parts of South America.

Ithomid Butterfly
(Pseudoscada sp.)
Here, the butterfly is drinking
through its angled proboscis from a
leaf's surface.

Butterfly
(Heliconis melpomena)
As well as feeding on nectar this
butterfly also eats pollen, grains of
which can be seen here sticking to
its curled proboscis. The protein
they contain may account for the
insect's unusual longevity.

ABOVE:
Green Katydid
(Family Pseudophyllidae)
At rest, the wings' apparent veining closely resembles that of a leaf, so that the mid-rib and veins of a green leaf camouflage the insect perfectly in an environment of living plants. If disturbed, the katydid's first line of defence is to flutter like a leaf blown in the breeze.

TOP:
Stink Bug
(Acanthocephala sp.)
Stink bugs – as their name indicates – are noted for their nauseating odour and taste which protect them from predators. Some species are themselves predatory although most, including this large type from Venezuela, suck the sap of plants.

ABOVE:
Cicada
(Family Cicadidae)
This close-up of a cicada's face shows the compound eyes on the side of its head and the lens-like ocelli centred between them.

6
Hunting Prey

It is dusk. A mouse possum is abroad on an evening snuffle. It has a long nose, soft brown fur and ears which appear rather too large for it. It creeps and scurries through the leaves of the forest floor searching for tasty insect morsels and the occasional worm. It is now too dark for the pit viper to see, but the heat-sensitive pits around its jaws guide it through the night with the accuracy of a slow, heat-seeking missile. In the growing darkness the warmth of the mouse possum's body appears as an infra-red glow as the viper moves towards its prey. The mouse possum pauses, its large ears twitching, but the snake remains motionless. The possum scuttles on, the snake lunges, and a toxin evolved over millions of years quickly does its work.

For some, the rainforest has a pervasive atmosphere of menace. It is filled with killers employing extraordinary stealth, speed and cunning, exploiting their world without notions of either mercy or greed.

Large predators, such as jaguars, patrol the forest floor at night, occasionally climbing up onto low treelimbs from which to drop down silently on a passing peccary or tapir. Smaller cats, such as the jaguarundi, ocelot and margay, are excellent climbers, and hunt small birds, mice and lizards in the branches of the forest. Not much is known about the lives of these predators because they are hard to track through the forest at night.

Encounters with snakes are equally rare, not because they are absent, but because they are invisible. Occasionally a snake will appear, sliding across a forest path or curled up in a bush above one's head, but generally they blend so well with their surroundings that it is quite possible to walk over one without ever seeing it. Ground-living snakes tend to be coloured in shades of brown, while those occupying the canopy, such as the emerald tree boa and the vine snake, are brilliant green. The cat-eyed tree snake hunts for frog's eggs beneath the leaves, gobbling them up like so much tapioca when it finds them. Some snakes search out lizards, others, bird's eggs, and some even lie in wait at night, to catch bats visiting flowers for pollen.

Birds are fine forest predators too, and none is more spectacular or rare than the enormous harpy eagle. These birds watch from tall emergent trees for sloths and monkeys. Swooping beneath the canopy on broad, sound-proofed wings, the harpy comes up beneath an unsuspecting animal, snatching it from its branch with upturned talons. In other great forests of the world there are similar big birds of prey, none larger than the monkey-eating eagle of the Philippines, which hunts flying lemurs as they glide from tree to tree on outstretched cloaks of skin. Smaller birds of prey quarter the forest understorey. The double-toothed kite follows monkey troops around, hoping to pick off the insects they disturb as they feed. Tiny hawks return time and again to the flowers where hummingbirds feed, and wait to snatch them.

Not all predators are large. Spiders and insects snare, poison, deceive and chase a multitude of meals both by day and night. There are wasps which kill spiders, praying mantises which disguise themselves as flowers, bugs which suck their prey to death, and parasitic wasps which lay their eggs in the brains of ants. Insects use a whole armoury of mechanisms to defend themselves, from beetles that squeak to alarm attacking birds to termites which have small 'guns' on their heads which shoot sticky fluid over their rivals.

Natural selection has given rise to remarkable camouflage which can be either aggressive, and intended to fool approaching prey, or defensive: intended to fool a passing predator. A mantis may therefore imitate a leaf, remaining invisible until its deadly limbs clutch a passing fly, while a moth may have evolved to mimic ostentatiously a bee or a wasp and so avoid being eaten. An extraordinary co-evolution has occurred, too, where animals appear to take advantage of each other to avoid predation. The oropendola, a large colourful bird which suspends its woven nest from tree branches, will often only build this nest in a tree also occupied by bees or wasps. Oropendola chicks are parasitized by botflies, which the bees keep away. At times when there are no botflies, the oropendolas hang their nests in any tree.

The trees of the forest are sometimes filled with a mixed hunting flock of small birds, darting among the leaves and branches and moving like a wave through the trees. The flock may comprise fifty species or more, searching the forest together for insects. Antwrens may occupy the top levels, while woodcreepers and ovenbirds work the trunks.

Many of the species which join these flocks, among them the brilliantly coloured vireos and flycatchers and the more drably attired warblers, migrate immense distances annually, delighting the eyes and ears of birdlovers in North America. As the rainforests of Central and South America are dwindling, so are the numbers of these migratory birds.

PREVIOUS PAGE:

Fer-de-lance
(Bothrops atrox)
A particularly venomous species,
up to two-and-a-half metres (eight
feet) in length, the fer-de-lance is a
member of the pit viper family.

Praying Mantis
(Acontiothespis sp.*)*
Dayflying Moth
(Isanthrene sp.*)*
Mantids lead a totally predatory
life, feeding voraciously on insects
and sometimes small vertebrates.
Most species are beautifully
camouflaged to match their
surroundings, allowing them to
stalk or lie in wait for their victims
without detection.

Here, the moth's remarkable
resemblance to a wasp, both in
form and colour, would normally
protect it from most larger
predators, but its colour warning
system does not work with other
insects who perceive different
wavebands of light invisible to most
vertebrates.

The Praying Mantis

Some of the most efficient predators in the forest are also the
smallest. None is more chilling than the praying mantis. Its
forelimbs are clasped together in front of its body with an air
of religious supplication when at rest, but if an unwitting
insect passes within range, they are transformed into a lethal
gin trap, sprung with breathtaking speed. Many mantises are
beautifully camouflaged, disguised as flowers or mottled in
order to disappear into the leaves from which they surprise
their prey. In some areas praying mantises capture tree frogs
and even small mammals. Reproduction is a hazardous affair,
the smaller male approaching the female with special care, as
she is inclined to devour him whilst in the act of copulation.
This is not a disaster for the species as the headless male
continues to mate while he is slowly eaten. The nerve cells
controlling the process are in the last segment of his
abdomen. Biologists have argued that, his job done, the male
merely provides a valuable food item which enhances the
female's chances of survival, and therefore those of her
offspring. Despite this gruesome habit, the females are doting
parents and stand guard over their egg masses until the tiny
nymphs hatch.

Jaguarundi
(Felis yagouaroundi)
This small, slender forest-floor cat
is about a metre to a metre-and-a-
half (three to five feet) long and
preys on small mammals and birds.
It can be found over a large area of
America, from Texas to Argentina.

OPPOSITE:
Ocelot
(Felis pardalis)
One of the most beautiful of cats,
the ocelot or painted leopard is also
one of the major mammalian
predators of the South American
rainforest. It is around a metre
(three feet) long, and is a solitary
hunter, preying on birds, lizards,
small mammals and fish. Its pelt is
highly valued by the fur trade and
in many areas it is endangered as a
result.

Long-Horned Grasshopper
(Family Tettigoniidae)
This insect rests during the day but
forages at night for smaller insects
and vegetation.

Spider
(Brachypelma vagans)
With a leg span of about thirteen
centimetres (five inches), this so-
called bird-eating spider is a
member of the sub-order
Mygalomorpha, which contains the
largest spiders in the world. It
preys chiefly on large insects,
although it will occasionally take
small birds and mammals which are
unfortunate enough to become
ensnared in its thick web.

Scorpion
(*Centruroides* sp.)
Scorpions are the most ancient of terrestrial arthropods, with fossil records dating back 400 million years. They are found in warm climates all over the world and are particularly abundant in tropical rainforests. However, they are rarely encountered as they are only active at night. This is a particularly dangerous species: its venom, a neurotoxin, is produced by glands at the base of the sting and causes paralysis of the cardiac and respiratory muscles.

Morelet's Crocodile
(*Crocodylus moreleti*)
With an armoury of tough scales and powerful jaws equipped with sharp interlocking teeth, crocodiles have strong advantages over their prey. They lie, invisibly, almost totally submerged, with eyes, ears and nostrils just breaking the surface. Morelet's crocodile is one of many endangered species.

OPPOSITE:
Epiphytes
These plants live on the branches of other plants and shrubs, but are not parasites. They derive all their nutrients from leaves and other debris that catch on these branches, and from the mist and rain.

LEFT:
Spectacled Caiman
(Caiman sclerops)
There are several species of caiman, and all are confined to Central and South America. Habitat destruction is endangering their survival.

BELOW:
Marine Toad
(Bufo marinus)
A cousin of the European toad, the marine toad may weigh as much as a kilo (two pounds). It lives on the ground and will eat any living creature that will fit into its wide mouth.

Giant Flatworm
(Geoplana gigantea)
The highly predatory flatworm is warningly coloured in black and orange. This one, measuring about fifteen centimetres (six inches), is in the process of slowly eating a giant, forty-centimetre (fifteen-inch) forest snail. The flatworm hunts slugs and snails, following the victim's slime trails then engulfing the prey through a mouth-like opening in the centre of its underside.

ABOVE:
Long-Legged Wolf Spider
(Family Lycosidae)
Resembling a fragment of
vegetation, a wolf spider lies in
wait. Rather than ensnaring their
prey, most wolf spiders chase
potential victims over the ground.

TOP:
Fly
(Neodohrniphora curvineris)
This parasitic fly of the phorid
family is about to lay an egg at the
base of the neck of a leaf-cutting
ant. The maggot will hatch and
develop inside the living ant and
eventually emerge as an adult,
leaving its host dead.

Fer-de-lance
(Bothrops atrox)
Agouti
(Dasyprocta)
The snake eats the agouti, a type of
forest rat, headfirst. Mosquitoes are
gathering around the snake's jaws
to suck its blood.

7
Camouflage

Life in a rainforest is not always what it seems. It is a place of subterfuge, advertisement, mistaken identity, and cryptic messages. In an environment where death stalks behind every leaf, it pays not to be seen for what you are. Conversely, to be a sheep in wolf's clothing may be a cunning way to steal up on a meal.

The rainforest plays to our senses. Its rich tapestry of colours, textures, and shapes provides many possibilities for camouflage if hunted creatures need to disappear. The browns of most of the bulky mammals blend into the forest background, and are only visible to the sharp eyes of the jaguar. Even brightly coloured birds somehow disappear when they come to rest. The three-toed sloth has fur with grooves, in which green algae grow, enabling it, when asleep, to appear like a moulding ants' nest hanging beneath a branch.

Insects have developed deception to a high level of artistry. The caterpillar of the swallow-tail butterfly has evolved precisely to mimic a fresh bird dropping. Shield bugs appear to avoid danger by clinging to the surface of leaves, indistinguishable from water droplets. And a day-flying moth exactly resembles a wasp while a katydid emulates the appearance of a decaying leaf on the forest floor.

Rainforests are the giant laboratories of the insect defence industry. Peering at a twig or leaf, it is almost impossible for our eyes to spot a green caterpillar lying along a stem, or a bug designed to appear as an innocent piece of fluff. To animals which are hunted by insectivorous birds, marauding predatory wasps, or a creeping praying mantis, even a degree of safety afforded by deception is sufficient evolutionary force, over millions of years, to result in quite remarkable adaptation for survival.

In this way the katydid's wing has been transformed through time to have dual functions of flight and trickery. Those katydids that live near to the ground have wings which resemble aged, brown leaves, complete with decayed holes and fine surface markings as detailed as Breton lace. Those that live on branches higher in the forest grow wings which are almost indistinguishable in colour, form and texture from the leaves which surround them. Antennae are positioned to appear like the leaf stem. If this disguise fails and a bird approaches for the kill, the aggressor is startled by what it still half-supposed might be a leaf, startlingly transformed into two enormous eyes, complete with iris and highlights. This flamboyant display might cause the bird to break off its attack for an instant, long enough for its prey to vanish into the background of leaves again.

Expert camouflage is not confined to insects. Glass frogs stand guard beside their egg masses to prevent predatory insects from attacking them, but are themselves appealing as food. To reduce their exposure, their bodies are exactly coloured to mimic the blobs of yolk and gel which make up the egg mass. Frogs in the canopy tend to be green but may hold colourful 'flags' beneath their bodies which can be deployed at will, when the coast is clear, to attract a mate. The mottled colours of many snakes are well known, but the eyelash viper is bright orange. This enables it to conceal itself in similarly coloured ripe fruit, the better to snatch passing diners. Subterfuge can take many forms. The ctenuchid moth so perfectly mimics a deadly wasp that few predators will touch it. Ants are numerous but are rarely preyed upon effectively so many insects, and some spiders, have evolved to resemble them. One spider, already closely resembling an ant, goes further and uses its extra pair of legs to wave in front of its head as ant-like antennae. To complete the imitation it moves with the jerky, inquisitive movements of its model as it scurries over the leaves.

Insects have had to evolve to deal with plant poisons, and many have turned this to advantage by storing the poisons in stinging spines. Predators soon learn not to tackle poisonous prey. Bright advertisement helps an inexperienced hunter to remember a distasteful meal, so many poisonous butterflies and caterpillars are memorably designed.

Butterflies with a latticework of black etched on their wings are often poisonous. Those with transparent wings usually occupy the understorey where the gloom favours the translucent structure. Those that live higher in the forest where dappled sunlight predominates are coloured in yellow and black lines, perhaps to benefit from the same measure of protection afforded to a tiger in similar light conditions. In the full glare of the upper canopy, orange or blue butterflies strongly contrast with the background but they almost vanish when entering shade, thus confusing a pursuer.

Orange and black heliconid butterflies are filled with passionflower poisons. Other poisonous species have evolved to mimic them so that they all benefit from being indistinguishable in the crowd. This Muellerian mimicry confuses predators, and the confusion is increased by Batesian mimics, which resemble the heliconid group, but are not poisonous at all. These butterflies have evolved not only to creep in under the protective umbrella of dangerous friends, but look like them too.

OPPOSITE:
Where the bulk of life is found in plants, animals have adapted themselves and use camouflage accordingly.

Spider
(Marxia sp.)
The spider has made its web across the blade of a leaf and has spun four parcels of food matter which look exactly like its own body. If a predator attacks there is thus only a one-in-five chance that the spider will perish.

Stick Insect
(Family *Phasmatidae)*
This insect is so cleverly camouflaged that it almost disappears against a background of moss.

PREVIOUS PAGE:
Geometrid Moth
With wings the shape and colour of dead leaves, this moth even has spots that look like fungus. If disturbed, it floats down to the forest floor from its perch on the tree, just like a falling leaf.

Hind wing of a Grasshopper
(Lophacris gloriosa)
Like many grasshoppers, this
species is well camouflaged when
at rest, but when seen in flight the
gaudy pink hind wings are vividly
evident.

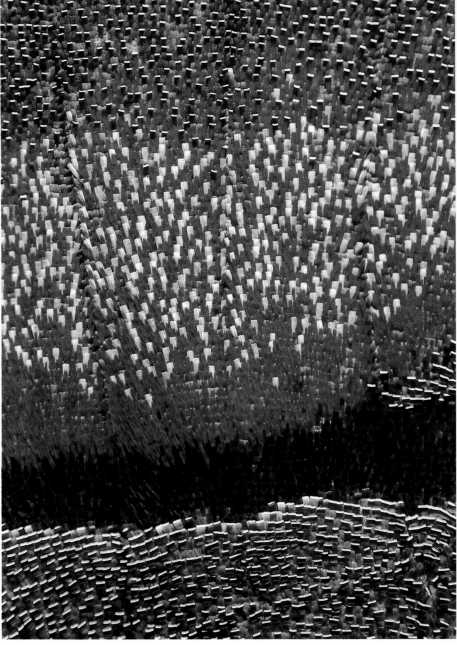

Wing of the Hairstreak Butterfly
(Thecla coronata)
A highly magnified view of the
underside hind wing.

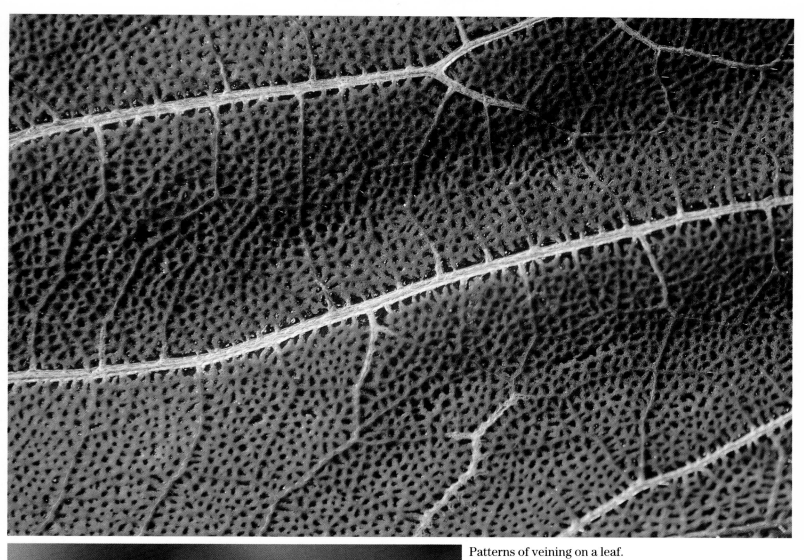

Patterns of veining on a leaf.

Eye of an Iguana seen in close-up.
(Iguana iguana)

Leaf-Hopper
(Angucephala mellana)
There are many thousands of
different species of leaf-hoppers
and they are found all over the
world. Like all bugs, their
mouthparts are designed for
sucking rather than biting or
chewing. This particular insect is
camouflaged to look like lichen.

Tent-Caterpillar Moth
(Family *Lasiocampidae*)
Settled for its daytime rest on
variously coloured lichens on a tree
trunk, this moth is perfectly
camouflaged.

TOP LEFT:
Cryptic Katydid
(Paraphidia sp.*)*
This katydid strongly resembles
the lichen on which it feeds.

TOP RIGHT:
Cryptic Saturnid
(Family Saturniidae)
The dappled light which sweeps
across the forest floor aids
camouflage.

ABOVE:
Moth
(Family Lepidoptera)
An unidentified cryptic moth. Like
many other insects illustrated in
this book, it was not possible to find
a specific name for this moth. The
rainforest abounds with creatures
that have no formal name and
identification: estimates vary
between ten and forty million. It
seems inevitable that most will be
extinct before such an
identification is made.

ABOVE:
Cryptic Moth
(Family Lepidoptera)
Drawing up its front legs to cover
its eye-spots and holding on with
its other four legs, this moth looks
just like a broken twig.

ABOVE:
Cryptic Ctenuchid
(Eucereon sp.)
This ctenuchid is camouflaged
against lichen on a tree trunk.

TOP:
Cryptic Katydid
(Paraphidia sp.)
Cryptic katydid at rest on a leaf.
The choice of background is clearly
crucial to camouflage, as few
animals can change their disguise
at will.

Praying Mantis
(Choeradolis sp.)
This creature is making its slow,
jerky way through epiphytes
growing on an ireartea palm.

RIGHT:
Green Heliconid
(Philaethria dido)
The delicate wing shades of green
and silver are a good disguise for
this butterfly against a background
of dappled light and green leaves.

Black Witch Moth
(Ascalapha odorata)
The female of the species at rest on
a shattered branch. With a
wingspan of about twenty
centimetres (eight inches), this
insect belongs to the same family
as the more familiar and modestly
sized owlets or noctuids.

Damselfly
(Euthore fasciata)
The dramatic black-and-white striping provides effective camouflage in the gloom of the understorey.

ABOVE:
Golden Tanager
(Tanagra arthus)
Close-up of wing feathers.

ABOVE RIGHT:
Bushmaster
(Lachesis muta)
The sloughed skin of a growing
snake.

Lantern Bug
(Fulgora laternaria)
Magnified eye-spot on wing.

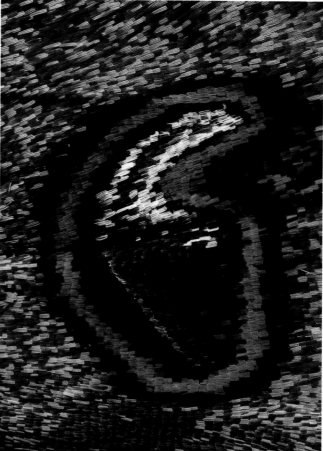

Widow Moth
(Erebus odora)
The eye-spot of this moth is
particularly subtly shaded, with a
highlight exactly like that of a
mammalian eye.

ABOVE:
Swordtail Butterfly
(Eurytides protesilaus)
Close-up of fore wing.

TOP:
Owl Butterfly
(Caligo beltrao)
Eye-spot on the underside hind
wing.

Texture

To a minute caterpillar the stem and ribs of a rainforest leaf
are like hills and valleys in which to hide, with flat plains in
between for grazing. Trees often produce their leaves from
the branches in small bunches or 'flushes', coloured in
attractive tones of red, purple and magenta. These can easily
fool the human eye into believing the tree is in flower. A close
look at the canyons and caves of tree bark between the
colonies of epiphytes reveals a host of creatures almost too
small to see, roaming through a miniature downtown
Manhattan. The textures and patterns of the inhabitants
themselves are incredibly rich. On close inspection the
surface of a butterfly wing breaks up into plates of pigment,
combining to produce an impression as skilful as that of a
Monet painting. Close up, a lizard's or snake's skin is
composed of scales which natural selection has fashioned
into a coat of many colours, which is as effective as the bright
plumage of some birds in signalling territory or claiming a
mate.

RIGHT:
Cryptic Katydid
(Paraphidia sp.)
The projections on the head and
the leaf-like mid-rib on this
katydid's wing help an effective
camouflage.

BELOW:
Jaguar
(Panthera onca)
Disguised by palm fronds, a jaguar
watches while itself remaining
almost invisible.

OPPOSITE:
Bushmaster
(Lachesis muta)
The snake is curled up motionless,
lower right of the picture, waiting
for prey beside a rodent run.

8
Reproduction

Trees in the rainforest must use a variety of pollen messengers to ensure that they are fertilized and that one generation follows another. The secret of how these great forests reproduce themselves remains one of nature's most enduring mysteries. Its complexity may also prove fatal, for if we do not discover how to regrow the rainforests they will gradually disappear.

To walk through a hectare of rainforest is to enter a laboratory of evolution filled with bizarre examples of sexual contracts between animals and plants. With no wind inside the forest and only infrequent squalls above it, the giant rainforest trees and the epiphytes which grow on their branches have evolved ways in which to attract insects, birds and bats to carry the pollen dust from flower to flower.

In an unseasonal forest, flowers are produced all year round by trees, epiphytes, vines, and a host of subcanopy shrubs. Some are large and showy, others minute and inconspicuous. Looking across the forest from a position high up in a tree it is sometimes possible to see huge areas of the canopy painted in a great blaze of a single colour, all white, perhaps, or yellow. These trees are 'big bang' strategists. They produce all their flowers together in a big show, attracting many small bees which move between the crowns gathering nectar and distributing pollen.

More often, the variety of species in a rainforest is so great that individuals of the same species may grow quite far apart. Trees therefore have had to develop special relationships with powerfully flying bees, bats and birds, who need to be capable of delivering pollen to the correct tree species a considerable distance away. This operation requires powerful incentives and reliable messengers.

To achieve success, plants have invented brightly coloured flowers, sweet scents, exotic nectars, and pollen rich in proteins. The purpose of these tools is to ensure that the plant's sperm, its pollen, is precisely delivered to the female flower parts of the same species. Many plants use large bees which 'trapline' through the forest, moving from one plant to another over distances of many kilometres. A large eulaema bee might have three different types of pollen on its abdomen, legs and head, each one belonging to a different plant species it regularly visits on the trapline, and each designed to match the collection mechanism of the recipient flower.

Rather than produce a mass of flowers over a short period, some plants produce a small number each day throughout their season. *Brownea rosa-de-monte* produces one or two starburst clusters of red flowers in the understorey each day just before dawn, specifically to attract hummingbirds. In the hours immediately after dawn, birds such as the white-tailed hermit materialize in front of them in a blur of iridescent wings. As their tongues flicker deep into the flowers, the tiny birds' head and breast feathers become dusted with yellow pollen from the long stamens. It is a race against time, because small trigonid bees compete for the same food supply, and cut into the base of the flowers, robbing them of nectar but without pollenating them. Many plants have an armour-plated bract at the base of each flower to protect it from attack, and the flowers are tubular in shape, exactly fitting the shape of the hummingbird which attends them. They provide copious amounts of weak nectar which supply the hummingbird's need for a high-energy fuel. Those flowers designed for bees provide less nectar, but it is sweeter.

The plants that attract bats are open at night and are often coloured white so that they can be seen more easily. Like bird-pollenated flowers, they also provide large amounts of nectar. Some even grow tough petals with hook-like projections, making it easier for the bats to grasp them with their wings and claws while they probe with long tongues for nectar inside. White, delicate flowers with very long tubes may be pollenated by a single species of hawk moth whose proboscis is exactly the correct length, fifteen centimetres (six inches) or more, to reach the nectar source at its base. As plant and pollenator evolve together, they become increasingly tied to each other's needs and in so doing exclude other less well-endowed moths, which may prove to be unreliable pollenators.

Some orchids manipulate pollenators around their flowers with elaborate mechanisms. Metallic trigonid bees are drawn to orchids to collect oily scents with which they define their territories and lure mates. It is not very different from the human desire for scent and aftershave. On approaching a bucket orchid, an attractive metallic male slips unexpectedly from a special landing stage into a bucket of fluid in which it quickly sinks. There is only one escape tunnel. As the bee scrambles out, it is trapped in the tunnel and a pollen blob is glued to its back. Only then is it released. On entering a second orchid of the same species, the process is repeated, but this time, as the bee makes its escape, its pollen packet catches on a special hook in the tunnel, and the fertilization process is complete.

Ithomid Butterflies
(Phyciodes sp.)
Both pictures show butterflies
mating.

PREVIOUS PAGE:
Blue-Hooded Euphonia
(Euphonia musica)
The female of the species inside
her nest. A member of the tanager
family, the blue-hooded euphonia
feeds on mistletoe seeds in the
canopy but nests in the sub-
canopy.

Frogs
(Gastrophryne pictiventris)
The onset of the rainy season triggers reproduction in many species of frog and toad, and, as the swamplands fill with water, a stunning chorus of amphibians' mating calls can be heard at night. Here two frogs are in amplexus – holding onto one another before mating. This species lays its eggs in water.

Mating

The rainforest is so rich in life that thousands of creatures may be competing to find a mate within a small area and so complex systems of territories, courtship displays, and contests of strength occur to ensure that the right pair find each other. Scents, sounds and signs are all used, usually with one sex being the signaller and the other the receiver. Male silk moths can track a female over four kilometres (two-and-a-half miles) away by sensing just a few hundred molecules of her sex pheromone on the breeze. Once found, pairs employ a new set of courtship rituals, using conspicuous patterns, antennae stroking, and wing or leg movements. Female insects sometimes shower their suitors with aphrodisiacs. The process of finding a mate can be fraught with difficulties. As each day the forest becomes more fragmented, individuals, particularly of the larger species, find it harder to meet one another, and so their numbers fall, until their gene pool is too small for a viable population to survive and they become extinct.

Red-Eyed Tree Frogs
(Agalychnis callidryas)
Tree frogs seen in amplexus. This species is well camouflaged during the day, lying flat and immobile with eye sockets contracted into its head. At twilight it wakes to supply a nocturnal chorus competing with that of the crickets and grasshoppers.

Tent-Making Bats
(Ectophylla alba)
A shelter built from a heliconia leaf is used as a daytime roost for an average of forty-five days. The bats chew away each end of the mid-rib of the leaf so that the blade drops down on both sides of the roosting area. They then roost in the hollow, clinging to the mid-rib with their back feet. White is an unusual colour for a bat but when the sun shines through the leaf they appear green and so are inconspicuous to predators.

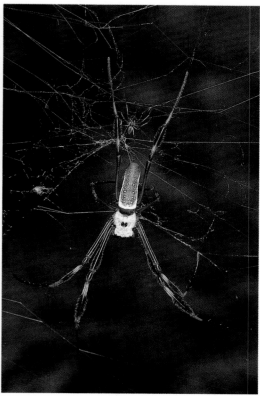

Spiders
(Nephila sp.)
The male of this species is so much smaller than the female that she does not eat him after mating, as many other spiders do. The male transfers his sperm to the female by sucking it up into his mouthparts and then injecting it into her.

OPPOSITE:

Tree Frog Tadpoles
(Hyla ebraccata)
Frogspawn laid in water can fall prey to aquatic predators, so this frog lays its eggs on leaves above the water, in this case on the swamp plant, *Spathphyllum* sp. They are safer here, and the hundreds of spawn masses laid during the night give each individual a better chance of survival, although they are still sought out by the leaf-climbing *Imantodes* snakes.

RIGHT:

Tree Frog Tadpoles
(Hyla ebraccata)
Still in their jelly, the tadpoles slide off the leaf into the water below. Once there, they wriggle away to swim free.

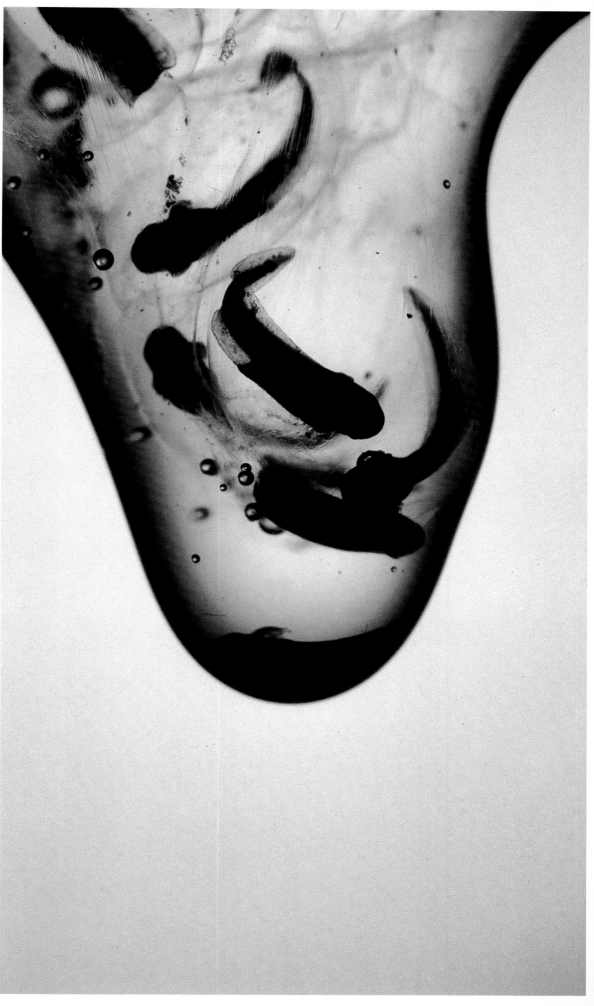

ABOVE:
Wax Flower
(*Anthurium* sp.)
Enshrouded in early morning mist, this bright-red flower stands out in the gloom of the forest floor.

TOP:
Orange Trumpet
(*Pyrostegia ignea*)

Violet-Eared Hummingbird
(*Colibri thalassinus*)
Hummingbirds need to visit thousands of flowers every day to extract enough nectar to survive. This bird is visiting the blooms of an erithrina bush. At night many of the smaller species save energy by lowering their metabolism to about one-fifth of its daytime value, effectively going into a brief hibernation.

OPPOSITE:
Keel-Billed Toucan
(Ramphastos sulfuratus)
The toucan is one of the most striking birds in the forest. A relative of the woodpecker, it is noisy, aggressive and brilliantly coloured. It is found only in the rainforests of Central and South America where it feeds chiefly on fruit. The bill is very light and ineffective for defending the bird despite its immense size.

RIGHT:
Orchid
(Oncidium sp.)
Many orchids have complex floral structures that have evolved to suit a specific insect on which the plant depends for pollenation.

Red-Eyed Tree Frog
(Agalychnis caladryas)
Having woken from its day-time roost on a bromeliad leaf, a tree frog embarks on a night of foraging and courtship.

Quetzal
(Pharomachrus mocino)
This spectacular bird frequents the Central American rainforests at high altitudes. It feeds on the wing, darting from perch to perch and hovering to catch insects and pick berries. It will also eat frogs and snails.

Stripe-Backed Wren
(Campylorhynchus sp.)
Most wrens have powerful songs
with intricate melodies that seem
too loud to come from such tiny
throats. Some tropical species
perform antiphonal duets, one bird
singing the first few notes of the
song and its mate completing it. As
both sexes sing throughout the
year, it is thought that this may be
the way in which pairs keep in
touch with one another in their
often impenetrable habitat.

9
The Upper Canopy

Behind every leaf, within each hollow tree, inside a million plants growing beyond our reach high in the canopy, are numerous micro-worlds in which small animals exist whose lives are scarcely known to us. The arboreal architecture of the rainforest provides a solid matrix for all the life in the forest. Some trees are vast, the tallest growing higher than a twenty-storey building. The ecology of the hidden world in their crowns remains nature's last biological frontier.

Unlike the largely bare branches of a temperate forest, those of rainforest trees are festooned with ferns, bromeliads, mosses, liverworts and lichens, which collectively are known as epiphytes. Even the waxy surfaces of individual leaves can sprout a veritable jungle of micro-epiphytes just millimetres high. Epiphytes, or air plants as they are often known, consist of some 28,000 species in sixty-five families, most of which are found in the great rainforests of America and South-East Asia. Only in America are bromeliads to be found growing side-by-side with arboreal cacti and orchids. In recent years, since scientists began exploring tall, inaccessible rainforest tree crowns with climbing ropes, walkways, and even hot-air balloons, the true importance of epiphytes to the rainforest community has been realized.

Lianas and vines, which do not have strong trunks, reach the energy-producing light of the canopy by supporting themselves on the trunks and branches of trees while keeping their roots firmly in the ground. Epiphytes have gone one stage further and have abandoned the earth altogether to colonize canopy branches with the help of flying animals or the wind. Some epiphytes produce light seeds, which float up into the canopy, whilst others pass through the guts of birds and are lodged there in droppings. Epiphytes are in effect botanical hitchhikers seeking a place in the sun.

Despite its location in some of the wettest parts of the world, the canopy is a dry place. Many epiphytes have the capacity to store water in fleshy roots and stems in a similar way to desert plants. The early morning mist which so often envelops the canopy is used by these plants to stay alive. Bromeliads, which are related to pineapples, go further and use their spiky leaves to channel rainfall and dew into the centre of the plant, which is shaped like a bucket of overlapping leaves. Here as much as ten litres (two gallons) of water may be retained. The spread of the leaves also captures debris falling from tree branches above. This then rots, providing those nutrients which the bromeliad cannot retrieve from the soil. Many epiphytes such as stagshorn and bird's nest ferns also obtain nutrients in this way.

The leaves, bird droppings, and the decaying bodies of creatures which have used epiphytes as their homes, combine to form a valuable nutrient source high above the ground. In addition, fine hairs on the epiphyte leaves sieve dust particles in the air, and capture nutrients dissolved in rain. Fully half the nutrients in the rainforest canopy foliage may be pirated out of the air and locked up into epiphytes in this way. Trees have turned this form of piracy to their own advantage and grow roots from their branches into the mineral-rich epiphyte garden, thus benefitting from this personal store before it falls to the ground where other competing trees may use it. So finely balanced is this scramble for scarce food supplies in the rainforest environment that some trees grow roots into their own trunks, or those of neighbouring trees, to tap their rotting cores. Most canopy giants are hollow. The droppings of the bats, snakes and owls which live inside serve to enrich the tree further, enabling it to outgrow neighbours and rivals.

Most remarkable of all is the way epiphytes are used as filling stations, homes and nurseries by the animals of the canopy. The abundant water supply in bromeliads provides passing monkeys or lizards with pools from which to quench their thirst. Female giant damselflies lay their eggs there, as do mosquitoes. Both hatch into aquatic larvae, the former feeding on the latter. After the giant damselfly larvae hatch into adults they fly like miniature helicopters through the forest, on four slow-beating, silvery wings, to search for nephila spiders' webs. These spiders may be as large as a human hand, but the damselflies attack them with impunity, snatching them from their webs and biting their bodies in half, discarding the head and legs and devouring the rest.

Bromeliads are also used as tadpole nurseries by certain tropical frogs. Marsupial frogs carry their eggs under flaps of skin on their backs, and when the tadpoles are ready to hatch, the frogs release them into bromeliads. Arrow poison frogs carry their tadpoles piggy-back-style up the side of a tree trunk and also release them into a bromeliad tank. This extraordinary display of parental care does not end here. Every day the female parent returns to the bromeliad and releases a single unfertilized egg into the water – a food parcel for her growing young.

Green-Winged Macaw
(Ara chloroptera)
Groups of these birds flying on
strong rapid wings high over the
canopy are an unforgettable sight
for visitors to the rainforest.
Macaws are monogamous and fly in
pairs within their flock.

Band-Tailed Guan
(Penelope argyrotis)
It has been suggested that the
preening oils in the bird's plumage
fix vitamin D when it basks in the
sun. Most guans are gregarious
birds and flocks of them line the
tops of forest trees where they feed
on fruit.

PREVIOUS PAGE:
These emergents are the tallest
trees in the forest, spreading
crowns as large as football pitches
above the canopy.

OPPOSITE:
Erythrina Tree
One tree houses a whole colony of crested oropendola birds. Their hanging nests are over a metre (three feet) long. The dominant male in the flock can be seen displaying, head down, high in the branches, from where it issues a melodious mating call.

RIGHT:
Howler Monkey
The monkey is shown in silhouette, resting in the late afternoon mist.

Green-Cheeked Amazon Parrot
(Amazonia viridigenalis)
Most of the twenty-five or so
species of amazons are stout-
bodied green parrots with short
tails.

　　Parrots are unique in that both
the upper and lower parts of the
beak, which are curved and
opposed, articulate. In other birds,
the upper mandible is fixed in the
cranium. Parrots also have strong,
grasping feet with two toes in front
and two behind.

OPPOSITE:
Common Squirrel Monkey
(Saimiei scivera)
About thirty centimetres (one
foot) long, this monkey travels in
groups, preferring scrub woodland
to deep forest, and feeds on
insects' and lizards' eggs.

Common Iguanas
(Iguana iguana)

Epiphytes
(Vriesea sp.)
The branches of rainforest trees, particularly those in the canopy, are festooned with bromeliads, ferns, mosses and orchids, all drawing their nourishment from the leaf-litter accumulated on the limbs.

Bromeliad Cricket
(Family *Gryllidae)*
This cricket lives in the canopy in and around bromeliads. When disturbed it runs down the bromeliad leaves into the tank of water in the central rosette. The minute water-repellent hairs that cover its body trap a layer of air for it to breathe while hiding.

Epiphytic Cactus
(Selenicereus grandiflorus)
The flower of this cactus measures twenty centimetres (eight inches) across. Its white colouring attracts pollenating bats after nightfall; by daybreak its petals have already withered and died.

Fragrant Orchid
(Encyclia fragrans)
As its name would indicate, and unusually for an orchid, this flower has a scent. Worldwide, there are over thirty thousand species of orchid, many of them living high in the canopy of the rainforest.

10
Decay and Renewal

There is a sense of timelessness when standing close to rainforest trees. A true primary forest may have stood for thousands of years and yet have seen just a few generations of large trees. Perhaps it is the apparent solidity that prevents us from comprehending that it is a constantly changing place.

All the forms of life in the forest eventually die and fall to earth, but nothing is wasted. The forest acts as a supremely efficient recycling system which depends on slim inputs of resources yet produces extraordinary rates of growth, an astonishing variety of species, and almost no waste. The forest engine runs on, sipping energy from the sun and oiled with tiny amounts of nitrates, phosphates and other minerals.

Old, leathery leaves coat the forest floor. Even before they reach the ground, the trees have drawn back vital minerals, sugars and salts until their chlorophyll green is mottled with yellows, reds and ochres. Some trees drop their leaves throughout the year, others do so in season. Once in the sunless understorey, an army of decomposers sets to work, living on the remains. Just below the litter of leaves there is a fine lacework of white fungal threads whose enzymes break down fallen leaves to mere skeletons in a matter of weeks. The hyphae of mycorrhizal fungi enter tree roots and draw sustenance from the sugar and nitrogen they contain, but in return the tree gains access to the vital minerals in the leaves before rain can wash them away.

Fungi have no need of sunlight, but they thrive on decay and the canopy giants would not live without them. But fungi remain almost invisible in the forest except when they reproduce, producing fine toadstools. Magenta mushrooms, yellow puffballs, orange candelabra and white stinkhorns each indicate a specific fungus. With little wind on the forest floor, many fungi use pungent odours to attract beetles or flies so that spores will be collected on their feet and carried to others of the same type.

A continuous rain of death from the branches above provides for many undertakers. An army of small beetles, ants, millepedes, woodlice, weevils and worms creep across the forest floor. Springtails leap from every upturned leaf, regiments of termites march abreast and the forest underworld seethes with microscopic life, scraping with tiny jaws and grinding the mighty forest trees to fine dust. Tiny ants scour the forest floor in search of insect carcasses which they dismember and carry back to their nests to seed with fungal spores. Unable to eat the tough insect shells, the ants feed on the crop of mushrooms instead.

Some ants have formed astonishing partnerships with plants. In the American tropics, *azteca* ants invade the rhizomes of tree ferns, while others inhabit bromeliads. In South-East Asian forests, *iridomyrmex* ants inhabit *myrmecodia* epiphytes and use their small chambers to store eggs and raise their young. They stream out of their host plants at night, returning with the carcasses of thrips, aphids, beetles and flies, and, back inside the plant, place them in micro-garbage dumps. The subsequent decay provides nutrients for the plant, and the ants get a safe home –a mutually beneficial arrangement.

To small insects on the forest floor there can be few greater terrors than an encounter with a hoard of marauding army ants. First come the sinister scrabbling sound of thousands of tiny clawed feet on dry leaves and a peculiar smell in the air. Army ants hunt in a front, at times thirty metres (one hundred feet) wide, and 600,000 strong, attacking cockroaches, katydids, beetles and even frogs caught in their path. Workers seize prey with large snapping mandibles and inject poison, at the same time releasing a pheromone spray which attracts others to the scene to help with the butchery process. Huge soldiers stand guard. Their jaws are even more impressive, and so strong that local Indians use the ants as sutures, forcing them to bite across a wound, then twisting off their bodies, leaving the jaws gripping the skin tightly together.

Birds, including the odd motmot, woodcreeper or cuckoo, follow the army ants in search of easy pickings, and one group, the antbirds, appear to forage exclusively by trailing these raiding parties. Huge tachinid flies also wait on nearby leaves, watching for escaping grasshoppers. They pursue an insect and plant an egg on its body, so that even though the grasshopper escapes the ants, the egg will hatch and burrow in, consuming its victim's body from the inside out. At dusk the army ants gather and create a bivouac for the night to protect their larvae and their queen, who feast inside on the gathered prey.

Despite such savage events, there is harmony here. Though the forest recycles itself, it remains enriched rather than impoverished. A small ant may help to plant a rainforest seed, the resulting seedling may wait many years for a gap in the canopy into which it can grow and termites may flourish within its fallen trunk half a century later. Everything you have read about here could be contained in a single acre of tropical rainforest. Each second of every day, another acre is consigned to history, burning brightly in the night sky.

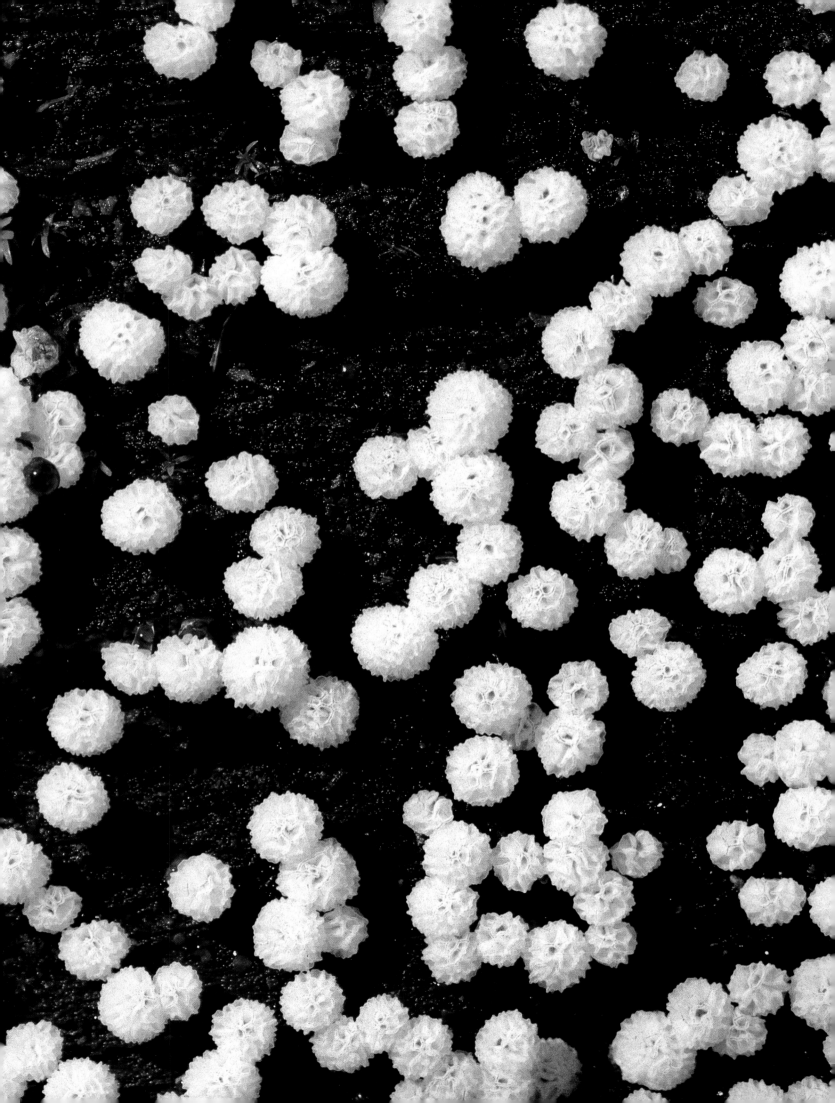

The Forest Floor

The crowns of giant rainforest trees contain the majority of
the life of the forest but most visitors are confined to the
forest floor, where there is nonetheless much to discover.
Those with eyes to look, and patience, will find a multitude of
surprises. Mammals such as deer, wild pigs, jaguars, agoutis
and pacas are better at watching us than we are at finding
them, but handsomely coloured frogs, spectacular
caterpillars, startling butterflies and the flashing wings of
birds are to be seen everywhere. Pausing at a brook, one can
watch picturesque butterflies seeking minerals in the dung of
animals that have stood there to drink, or catch the silvery
gleam of tiny fish exploring the shallows. Peering into the
huge buttressed flanks of a tall tree, one might see squadrons
of delicate crane flies doing frenetic press-ups, or a praying
mantis disguised as a leaf. The underside of a leaf beside a
stream may reveal a cluster of glass frog eggs. The frogs lay
them here to avoid the appetites of fish and predatory
shrimps in streams. On hatching, the tadpoles fall into the
water, already better equipped to avoid capture than the
passively floating eggs.

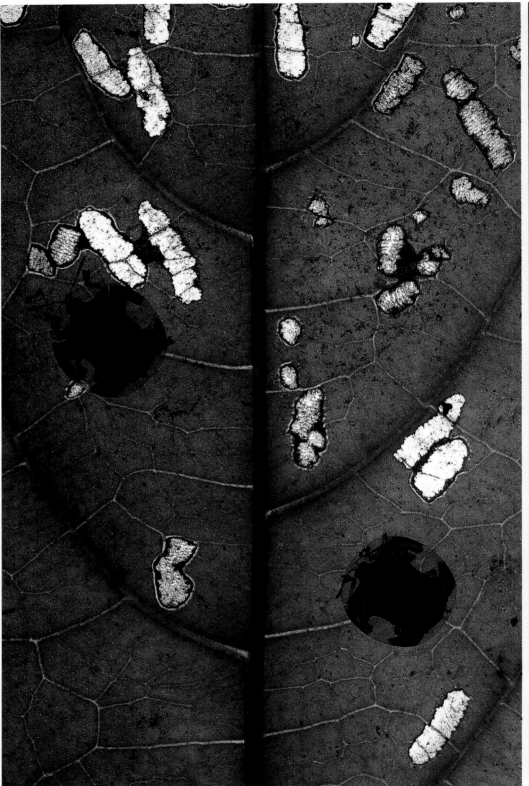

Tortoise Beetles
(Chariodotis vitreata)
Many of the tropical tortoise
beetles are brightly coloured and
iridescent. Here a pair are seen
feeding under a leaf.

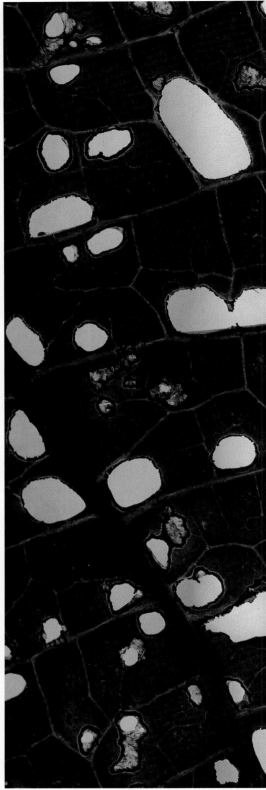

Very few leaves in the forest are
immune to attack from insects.
This one has played host to
chrysomelid beetles.

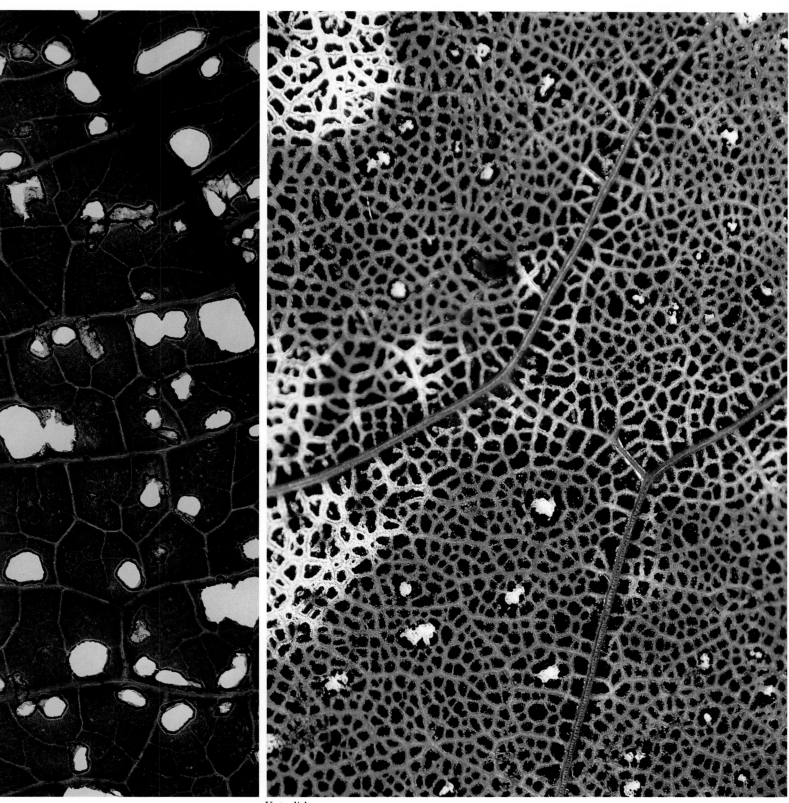

Katydid
(Paraphidia sp.)
Not only do the veins on the wing of this katydid imitate those of a leaf, but they also copy the brown patches of decay.

Termites
(Nasititermes corniger)
Worker termites expand their nest by adding their own excreta to reconstituted wood. The longer-nosed termites in the picture are soldiers standing guard, ready to squirt repellent chemicals through their noses at intruders such as ants.

Piper Infructescence
(Piper culebranum)
This plant, of the same family as the pepper, grows many fruits on one stem. *Ectatomma ruidum* ants are collecting its sweet fruits to store at their nest for food.

Tropical Stinkhorn
(Phallus impudicus)
Many plants produce 'putrefying' scents to attract insects which will help in the dispersal of their spores. Here, a tropical stinkhorn is covered with flies.

Heliconid Butterfly
(Heliconius antiochus)
This heliconid is preparing to roost under a twig. Species in the genus roost in groups. One theory proposed for this is that, as a group, their smell is stronger and predators, who associate it with distastefulness, stay away.

Owl Butterfly
(Caligo eurilochus)
Just as there are day-flying moths, there are night-flying butterflies. The huge owl butterfly, like its namesake, becomes active at twilight – this one is sheltering from the tropical rain under a fallen cecropia leaf.

The Cicada

After anything up to thirteen years below ground, sucking sap from the roots of trees with its piercing mouthparts, a cicada nymph tunnels its way through to the surface and transforms into an adult. After the immense effort of escaping from its nymphal case, the cicada rests for a time, while its wings harden, before flying off into the forest. The adults also feed on sap and have the ability to pierce even bark. They are best known for the remarkably loud calls with which the males attract females. On each side of the cicada's abdomen is a small convex plate which is thin and extremely elastic. This drum is pulled inwards by a small muscle which causes it to buckle, making a click, which is repeated when it is released. Some types of cicada can click up to a thousand times a second in this way. There are so many species of cicadas that they must divide the day into shifts, different species calling at different times, often with very distinctive sounds. Females, attracted to the incessant buzzing, sidle up to the males, signalling approval with their wings. A staring match may then ensue and continue for hours until, with some unseen signal, they move to complete their love dance.

Cicada
(Family *Cicadidae*)
After spending years underground living off the juices of tree roots, a cicada nymph sees the light of day for the first time as it emerges to metamorphose into an adult.

Cicadas are the noisiest of all the insects, the two thousand or so species known generating a vast range of different sounds.

A new shoot pushes its way up through the leaf litter on the forest floor.

OVERLEAF:
Rubicaeae leaf bud
(Pentagonia macrophylla)

What You Can Do

Above all, do not remain indifferent. The rainforest touches all our lives in ways that are not obvious. The money we deposit in high-street banks may find its way into loans used to build dams or roads far away, which may in turn cause the destruction of pristine rainforest. The forest enters our lives without our being aware of it – on our dinner tables in exotic fruits, nuts and vegetables; in the timber, such as mahogany, used in our furniture, windows and doors; in the drugs doctors use to fight disease; and in the germplasm with which farmers must revitalize domestic crops. It can be hard to appreciate even worthy causes from a distance, but as eco-tourism becomes a new driving force for travellers in the 1990s, more and more people want to see the world as it still is, and not as some man-manufactured spectacle. The next decade will finally decide the fate of the world's tropical forests. Issues of the environment have become part of mainstream political, business and scientific thinking. The advent of Green consumerism allows everyone to play a part, however small, by choosing products which do not harm the environment and which can be produced on a sustainable basis – and this applies to rainforest products too. There is usually some small additional cost, but one can think of it as insurance for the planet: a premium on a kind of environmental security policy.

The four important organizations listed below offer you opportunities to help save the rainforests in various different ways. Their addresses follow, together with those of other organizations in a number of countries which are actively involved in rainforest conservation:

Earthwatch

Earthwatch sends thousands of paying volunteers of all ages and walks of life out into the field to work alongside scientists, acting as their assistants. It is the only major organization which enables you to live for two weeks in a rainforest actively helping to solve some of the critical problems which you have read about in this book. No special skills are required other than enthusiasm and a willingness to learn. Earthwatch can match volunteers with scientists all over the world needing their help.

Friends of the Earth

This pressure group takes a radical approach to rainforest conservation and produces excellent information on the progress of rainforest destruction, consumer products to avoid, and ways of taking independent action to influence business and government both in your own country and abroad. FoE needs your help to keep the rainforest issue in the public eye.

Survival International

With its American sister organization, Cultural Survival, this group has championed the rights of indigenous forest people for many years. They provide regular bulletins, keeping you in touch with the plight of threatened rainforest tribes all over the world, and will help you to contribute financially to their protection wherever it is needed.

The World Wide Fund for Nature

This is the largest independent conservation organization in the world. The WWF is active in helping to manage rainforest nature reserves in many countries and specializes in accurate surveys, and in working with governments to create long-term projects. Turn to them if you would prefer to lend your support directly from home to those whose experience enables them to do the active work most effectively.

Rainforest Action Groups

AUSTRALIA

Campaign to Save Native Forests, 794 Hay Street, Perth, W.A. 6000.

Earthwatch Australia, Suite 3, Level 2, 283 George Street, Sydney 2000.

Friends of the Earth (Australia), 4th floor, 56 Foster Street, Surrey Hills, N.S.W. 2010.

World Wide Fund for Nature, Level 17, St. Martin's Tower, 31 Market Street, Sydney, N.S.W. 2000.

BRAZIL

ADFG – Amigos da Terra, Rua Miguel Tostes 694, 90.000 Porto Allegre.

Friends of the Earth, Funatura, Fundacao pro natureza, caixa postal 02–0186, 7001 Brazilia.

CANADA

Friends of the Earth, Probe International, 100 College Street, 6th floor, Toronto, Ont. M5G 1L5.

Friends of the Earth/Les Amis de la Terre, 251 Laurier Avenue W., Suite 701, Ottawa, Ont. K1P 5J6.

World Wide Fund for Nature, 60 St. Clair Avenue East, Suite 201, Toronto, Ont. M4T 1N5.

FRANCE

Les Amis de la Terre, 15 rue Gambey, 75011 Paris.

Association Technique des Boix Tropicaux, 8 rue du Colonel Moll, Paris.

Fundation Cousteau, 25 Avenue Magram, 75017 Paris.

ITALY

Amici della Terra, Via del Sudario 35, 00186 Rome.

MALAYSIA

Friends of the Earth, World Rainforest Movement, International Secretariat, 87 Cantonment Road, Penang 10250.

NEW ZEALAND

Royal Forest and Bird Protection Society of New Zealand Inc., P.O. Box 631, Wellington.

UK

Earthwatch Europe, Belsyre Court, 57 Woodstock Road, Oxford OX2 6HU.

Friends of the Earth, 26–28 Underwood Street, London N1 7QJ.

Living Earth, 10 Upper Grosvenor Street, London W1X 9PA.

Royal Geographical Society, Kensington Gore, London SW7.

Survival International, 310 Edgware Road, London W2 1DY.

World Wide Fund for Nature, Panda House, Weyside Park, Godalming, Surrey GU7 1XR.

USA

Cultural Survival, 11 Divinity Avenue, Cambridge, Mass. 02138.

Environmental Defense Fund, 1616 P Street NW, Suite 150, Washington D.C. 2003.

Nature Conservancy, 1800 North Kent Street, Arlington, Virginia 22209.

Natural Resources Defense Council, 1350 New York Avenue NW, Washington D.C.

Rainforest Action Network, 301 Broadway, Suite A, San Francisco, CA 94133.

Sierra Club, 730 Polk Street, San Francisco, CA 94009.

World Wide Fund for Nature, 1250 24th Street NW, Washington D.C. 20037.

WEST GERMANY

Friends of the Earth, Robinwood, Poseldorf Weg 17, 2000 Hamburg.

Index